Nighttime Fantasies
and
Bed Time Romance

By

Chrystine Dier

ISBN: 0-75965-162-0

This book is printed on acid free paper.

1stBooks – rev. 07/03/01

TABLE OF CONTENTS

INTRODUCTION

These stories are intended for anyone to enjoy. Each story is based in love and lust. Each story is based on couples in love. Each couple has an insatiable desire for each other, and the desire to please each other. A friend once told me that everything done in the bedroom is sacred as long as it is between two consenting adults. Well, these bedrooms are very sacred places.

I started writing my stories to express moments in time that are shared between two people that are so consumed by each other that they could, as the old folks say, "love so much they could drink your bath water". I wanted to put into words those things that we fantasize about having done. I wanted to tell stories that warmed you up late at night before your lover came home. I wanted to tell a story that had you wanting to call your lover and tell them to come home early. I wanted to tell stories that heightened the sensual feelings you never knew you had.

I dreamed of this little book staying by your bed and you could read it to your lover or ask them to read it to you as foreplay. I envisioned my stories being read over the phone to a lover as in Phonesex.

However you enjoy my stories, I hope you do enjoy my stories. They are from my heart, my dreams and my fantasies.

ANNIVERSARY

This is a story about a "She" and a "He". They could be any one of us, at any time in our lives. Their love and actions are independent of time or place. Here's their story according to me.

It was February 14th, the 15th anniversary of the consummation of their attraction and her love. Their relationship had been one of many ups and downs. "She" always felt as if she loved him more than "He" would ever know, more than "He" could comprehend. Her love was unconditional. "She" loved him while "He" was with other women, and through the many phases of his life, and it's changes. Many called her stupid, but "She" believed that if you loved someone it was with all of your heart, mind, body and soul.

Now, "She" was no saint. "She" had her share of indiscretions. There were other men in her life during his times of neglect. There was a child conceived and given birth to that was by another man, during one of his long absences. Through it all, "She" wanted only him.

They had come to a point in their relationship where they got together, spent time together, made love and went their separate ways. "He" was having his cake and eating it too. "She" was always hungry for more. Their times together continued in this manner through their 13th and 14th years. It was at the acknowledgment of this being the 15th year that "She" decided things were going to change.

Two weeks before, "She" began to put her plan into action. "She" mailed him an invitation to meet her at their spot on the night of their 15th anniversary. It read:

Let's spend some time together.
We'll sip a little wine
We'll do little a bump and grind.
We'll let our minds and bodies unwind,
As we let our hearts intertwine.
Meet me at our special place.
You know the time, so don't be late.
Our union is destined by fate.

"She" bought the slinkiest red, satin negligee for herself, and silk boxers for him. There was a "Before and After" bath accessory gift pack which contained a sensuous bubble bath for two, edible fruit flavored body paints, loofa scrub and mitts and massage oils. "He" bought a magnum of Dom Perignon, crystal flutes and a dozen red and a dozen white long stem roses. They both anxiously awaited their special night.

On their special night "She" was the first to arrive. "She" felt aroused, and her senses were heightened in anticipation of things to come. "She" had a few surprises up her sleeve, and was electrified by the power she felt. Her hair and makeup were perfect, and she seemed to glow. Her body ached for the passion she knew was to come.

"He" arrived shortly after her. "She" had time to light the room with candles and fill the Jacuzzi. "She" greeted him in her red satin negligee. "He" placed his packages on the floor to embrace her. "He" wrapped his big, strong arms around her body. "She" could feel the strength of his hands as they caressed her back. Her nipples hardened at the contact with the rough surface of his jacket. "He" kissed her full lips and tasted the sweetness of her tongue. His kisses moved across her jaw line and down her neck. "He" could feel the rapid pace of her pulse in her throat.

"She" slipped her hands under his jacket to begin opening the buttons of his shirt. The warmth and fragrance of his skin was making her loose control. The blood rushing from her brain to her center of womaness sounded like an ocean's roar. "She" knew she had to regain her control if she was going to win.

To break the ice "She" said, "To steal a line from Mae West, Do you have something in your pocket or are you just happy to see me?" "He" chuckled and stepped away as he rolled a nipple between his fingers. "He" knew that made her hot. "She" asked, "What did you bring with you?" "He" said, "Some Dom and roses." "She" told him, "Why don't you get undressed and I'll take care of the roses and chill the champagne. You'll find something more comfortable hanging in the bathroom."

With that he got undressed as "She" put the champagne in the ice bucket and set out the glasses. "She" admired the fine crystal of the glasses. "He" always had the best taste. The roses were in full bloom and were the deepest red and the most pure white "She" had ever seen. "She" arranged the roses by the Jacuzzi and then added the sensuous bubbles to the water. As the bubbles began to grow "She" slipped out of her negligee and slid into the warm churning water and waited on her lover.

"He" stepped out of the bathroom in his silk boxers. "He" was magnificent. The muscles in his chest and arms rippled with his every move. "He" had a very big and hard present inside of his boxers for her. Her mouth watered in anticipation. When "He" saw her sitting in the Jacuzzi surrounded by bubbles and her skin glistening from the moisture, his mouth dropped. Her eyes glittered from the knowledge of the power she had over him.

"Now get even more comfortable and come join me." she said to him. "He" moved as if in a trance. As "He" slid the elastic waist over his firm, round buttocks, "She" could feel her own juices stirring. "He" stood before her with his erection firm and at attention. "She" reached up out of the water to grasp the shaft of his penis. She guided him to her with her grip. "He" stepped over the edge into the water with her. "She" took him into her mouth, as if she were starving for his taste. The pleasure she gave him made his knees weak. "He" was forced to sit on the edge of the Jacuzzi as "She" worked her magic with her lips and tongue. "He" reached forward to caress her breast and "She" evaded his advances. "She" shook her head no. "He" said, "But baby I want to touch you." "She" again shook her head no.

"She" moved between his thighs and replaced her mouth with her breast. "She" surrounded his pulsing cock with her voluptuous wet breast and stroked him up and down with them. "He" began to moan her name. It started as a rumble in his chest and sprang from his lips of it's own volition. "She" felt even more powerful with his inability to control himself. (You see, "He" is usually a very silent and controlled lover.) "He" tried to caress her under the water. "She" could feel him try and find the hair that covered her point of intense pleasure. "She" backed away and told him, "I'm not ready for you to touch me yet." "She" was lying because the power she felt from arousing him and the control she possessed was a heady aphrodisiac. "She" could feel a warm tightening in her vagina. "She" truly ached for his touch, but she longed to be the one that orchestrated this nights events.

"She" stood up and guided him up with her. Her knees were weak with desire. "She" leaned against him and pressed her full nude, wet body against his. His erection pressed into her abdomen. "She" ran her hands from his shoulders, down his back, to his ass and pressed him into her. "He" wrapped his arms around her and held her tightly. "He" was happy just to be able to touch her.

"She" looked him in the eyes and then gave him a long, hot, passionate kiss. "He" tried to deepen the kiss and she ended it. "She" said, "Let's climb into bed. We can come back to the water after we have some fun." "He" followed her to the waterbed. "She" laid him down and then she lay on top of him. "She" held his hand above his head as she kissed him. "He" was so aroused he could not think. "He" was not used to her leading, it had always been him in the past. "He" never knew it could be so sexy. As he was having these thoughts he didn't notice her tying satin ropes around his wrists attached to the headboard. When he noticed that he couldn't move his hands it was too late and he was restrained. He opened his eyes with a start and asked, "Baby? What is this for? What do you think you're doing to me?" She smiled and said; "Now it's my turn to be the boss. I've been fantasizing about being in control and having you as my prisoner." He tried to struggle against his ties with no success, they only got tighter. She told him, "It's no use. I've been practicing my knots for two weeks. You only get freed when I'm ready."

She straddled his waist and kissed his lips. She told him, "Just lay back and enjoy." She could feel the tension in his body as he resisted the urge to fight her. She gave each of his nipples a kiss and a lick. She watched them respond to the attention by getting hard. She left his nipples and ran her tongue down the middle of his chest to his navel. She dipped her tongue into his navel and swirled it around and out. She heard him moan through the fog of her own arousal. Her pubic hairs grazed the shaft of his penis as she moved down his body. He was moaning her name and asking her to let him make her feel as good as she was making him feel. She just ignored him and continued on her path.

She was tempted to straddle his penis right then, but she wanted to make it last. She could feel the heat and wetness in her vagina. She ached for him, but the desire to control was stronger. She wanted to make him want her and ache for her as much as she has ached for him. She wanted to make him suffer as he waited.

As her mouth moved toward his erect penis his hips seemed to move off the bed. It was as if he was trying to rush the moment that she took him into her mouth. He knew how weak she was when it came to his dick. He knew that her mouth watered at the thought of licking him. In an effort to show him who was the boss, she moved past his dick and kissed his right inner thigh and then the left one. She heard him let out a moan as if he were in agony, and yet he opened his thighs as if asking for more. She was very tempted to go back to his thick shaft, but denied herself in favor of more torture.

She could tell he was enjoying himself in spite of himself. He writhed on the bed and begged her for release. She just moved down his legs with a sensual massage. When she got to his feet she worked her way up to his penis. She took him in her hand and stroked him up and down. She always loved the soft, silky feel of the skin on his dick. She used a firm grasp, which he always liked and he responded with a slow gyrating motion of his hips. She couldn't hold back anymore and she ran her tongue up the underside of his shaft. Her nipples grazed the top of his thighs. She didn't know if she could wait much longer herself.

As she took his whole penis into her mouth He moaned as if in agony. "Oh Baby. That feels so good. Let me make you feel good. Let me make you come." Those words were so tempting to her, but her desire to be in control was stronger. She stopped sucking his dick just long enough to tell him, "I'll say when it's time for you to make me feel good." She returned to her original task of making him almost come. As she worked on his erection she tasted his pre-come on her tongue and she stopped. She moved up to his chest and lay on top of him nipple to nipple.

"Why are you doing this to me?" he asked, slightly out of breath with passion. She responded with a smile and said, "I have always felt like the twist and turns of our relationship have been at your whim. I never felt as if I had any control. Well what I realized was that over the years I gave you my power and now I'm taking it back."

She then sat up and straddled his penis. She loved the feel of him sliding into her. She was so wet that she was ready for a long night of lovemaking. She rode him as she played with her own nipples. She closed her eyes and concentrated on giving herself pleasure. She could feel the tightening that was the beginning of a good orgasm. It made her ride him even harder. She never heard his moans of pleasure or words of encouragement. It was all for her. The harder she worked the better it felt. She was stretched to a fevered point of no return. She was almost there. Just a little bit more. Just a little bit more; and ... then... she ... came. Her body shivered all over as she slowed her pace.

She looked down at him and just as she focused on his face she could see the agony and she heard the words of him begging her to please help him. "Baby please don't leave me like this. It's our anniversary. Let's celebrate it together. I love you." She leaned forward and kissed him. She had thoughts of leaving him as he was and going home, but what she realized was that he had power over her because she loved him and she had power over him because he loved her. With that thought she kissed him again, untied his hands, and proceeded to give the man she loved the pleasure they both deserved.

AROMATIC LOVE

The bedside light gave the room a warm intimate glow. Caryn was snuggled in bed reading her Guide to Aroma Therapy with a diffuser blend permeating the air. She had combined clary sage, sandalwood, lavender and chamomile essential oils for serenity. Babyface played on the CD player and Caryn was wearing her favorite loungewear.

She was looking for an aromatic aphrodisiac, something to increase sensuality. She wanted to have the house and her body saturated with the scent of essential oils that would make her irresistible to Andre'. If she found the right combination, she could create a bath blend, diffuser blend and massage oil.

She always looked forward to the massage part of the night. She loved to touch Andre's skin and feel his muscles ripple under her fingertips. To feel his heart beat increase under her palm as she moved closer to his erection was a powerful feeling. Just thinking about it made her nipples harden. She wanted to get him so aroused that he was harder than he could remember. She wanted to make it hard for him to stay in control. She wanted it to be good enough to make him want lose control and all inhibitions. She wanted to make him want to make love all night long.

Their sex life was great, but Caryn always enjoyed adding something new. The love they shared kept the spark in their relationship, and she could honestly say that they were friends and shared many common interests, which gave the relationship strength. Andre' appreciated her enthusiasm and enjoyed the new things she brought to their relationship. How could he complain when he benefited from her efforts?

9

Caryn turned the pages and found the group of essential oils that were just what she needed. With just the right amounts of a little of this and a little of that, she could expect a night to remember. If this worked she could share it with her friends, and maybe get a side business going.

Caryn planned to have the bath ready for André when he came home. Candle light, essential oils and warm water would work wonders. She was going to have the diffuser in the bedroom with the massage oil waiting. She could hardly wait for him to come home. He was sure to be tired from a long day on the job. He was a city police officer and chased the bad guys all day. Caryn wanted to chase away his fatigue and invite his arousal to bed. She was sure a bath for two and then a massage was just what he needed.

Caryn went to her collection of essential oils and referred to her cookbook of aromatherapy. She was looking for just the right combination. She saw aromatherapy as a way to suggest the proper mood to the mind. It had been proven that the sense of smell was a powerful way to communicate to one's spirit, mood and mind. She found a recipe for an aphrodisiac. She needed to combine jojba, neroli, sandalwood, benzoin, jasmine, rose and vetever essential oils. If worn as a fragrance, it was suppose to excite the one who wore it as well as the one who got close enough to smell. There was a recipe for bath oil that would add to the passion. Caryn thought she had found just what she needed.

She got to work combining just the right amount of each ingredient. By the time she was expecting André to come home she had taken a bath in the bath blend and put some of her personal blend at all her pulse points. André came in the front door just as she was lighting the last candle around the bathtub.

"Hey baby. What's going on?" André said as he stepped into the bedroom. Caryn was standing by the bed in his favorite robe. It had an oriental design and was just short enough to show a hint of her ass. He walked toward her, kissed on the lips and wrapped his arms around her as he rubbed her skin through the satin fabric of her robe. He looked over her shoulder at the candles around the room. "Mmmm. You smell good." as he nuzzled her neck.

Caryn felt her nipples harden and her skin tingle as André nuzzled her neck and rubbed her skin. It seemed as if the aromatherapy was working she thought, as she felt his erection through his pants. She stroked his dick through his pants and felt it get harder against her hand. André started to release the ties of her robe. Caryn stopped him and said, "Wait baby. I have something for you in the bathroom." André continued to work the knot in her belt and said, "I have all I need right here in front of me if I could just unwrap it." "No baby. Let me get you undressed and let's go in the bathroom. Or better yet, why don't you get undressed and join me in the bathroom." With that Caryn walked towards the bathroom door. She walked in and dropped her robe on the floor as she shut the door.

André removed his clothes quickly and went to the bathroom. As he entered he smelled the scent from her skin even stronger. It seemed to make his head fuzzy and his dick harder. The room was steamy and his vision was distorted by the candlelight. Caryn was in the tub and candles surrounded it. "Why don't you come and join me?" André looked at her breast glistening from the water and could see her nipple. He said, "Why don't I just make you come?"

Caryn made a sound like a moan and a growl in her throat. He knew he was getting to her as he stood in front of

11

her with his dick hard and in her face. Andre knew she had a weakness for that part of his body. He didn't mind of course. Hell, he benefited from her desires. She loved to suck him until he came and he loved for her to do it. She had just the right amount of softness and hardness to her touch. Her tongue felt like it was giving his manhood a massage. She could take in enough of him into her mouth to make him lose control. She knew his spots that added to the pleasure. Just thinking about it was making him hornier.

Caryn seemed to regroup as he was becoming distracted by his desire. She realized that the aromatherapy was getting to her too. "Just get in the tub and see what I have in store for you." With that he joined her in the tub. The water was perfect. It was warm and soothing. He sat across from her and their legs were intertwined. The tub was one of the reasons that made them decide on the house, it was just right for two. "Come here." André said as her reached out for her. Caryn repositioned herself in the tub to sit between his legs and he wrapped his arms around her. He cupped her breast, one in each hand and squeezed each nipple. Caryn squirmed between his thighs and pressed her ass into his erection. With her voice husky from desire, she said, "Mmm Baby. You know how I like that. I want to fuck you all night long." Caryn turned around in the tub to face André. She kissed him and slid her tongue in his mouth. She wanted to feel his dick pumping in and out of her like her tongue was doing to his mouth.

André stopped the kiss and said, "Shit girl, I need you now. Let's get out of this water and get in the bed." Caryn had no protest and stood to step out of the tub. André reached up to slide his finger into her wet pussy and slid it in and out. Caryn almost fell back into the tub with the rush to her head from the arousal. She stood still for a moment enjoying the sensation and then said, "Come on baby. I don't want to wait any more."

They both got out of the tub. As the water spilled over the sides the candles were put out. André lay in the bed on his back with his dick standing at attention like a drunk solider, leaning a little to the side. Caryn walked to him and kneeled between his legs to grasp his dick. She leaned forward and took him into her mouth. All the way to the base and back up. Andre's thigh muscles tightened as he lay there enjoying her. She sucked the head of his penis and then licked the underside of his dick with her tongue from base to tip. André began to try and reach for her. "Come here baby. I want to be inside of you."

Caryn couldn't resist any longer. She had great plans for a massage, but that would have to wait. If she didn't have him inside of her soon she thought she would die. She sat up and slid up the front of his body and until they lay chest to chest. André kissed her and slid his tongue into her mouth. Caryn sucked it like she longed to suck his dick. She then pushed up and sat up straddling his waist with her thighs. She lifted up onto her feet and moved back over his dick. André guided himself into her with his hand. Caryn slid down onto his hard dick. They fit like a hand in glove. She settled down on him and then leaned forward to rest on her hands. She started to ride him, guided by her passion and desire to please the both of them.

She rode him and slid up and down, with his dick going in and out. He was moaning her name and she his. "Caryn. Oh Caryn, Baby it feels so good to be inside of you. You feel so good." "André I love to feel you inside of me. I love the way you fit inside of me." The pace quickened. Caryn could feel her insides tighten up like a top being wound up. She was about to come. Andre' quickened his pace. Caryn knew he was about to come. She ran her tongue up his chest and kissed his lips. She slid her tongue into his mouth and pulsed it in and out of his mouth at the same rate as his dick in and out of her. She could feel his moan vibrate through her tongue. Caryn ended the kiss and said, "Baby...I'm...about...to...come. Mmmm baby. You make me feel so good. Oh, Baby! Oh Andre! Andre!" And just as she was coming, so was he. Andre called out her name over and over as each spasm of his orgasm ran through his body.

Caryn lay spent on his chest with him still inside of her. She could feel his heart beat in her own chest. "That was so good. I had intended to give you a massage, but I need a nap first" "I know what you mean. You and your sexy ass are always draining me of my energy." Caryn rolled off of his chest to snuggle into the crook of his arm. He looked over at her and said, "Baby, every day that I am with you makes me realize that I love you more and more. Don't ever change the special woman that you are." Caryn looked at him and said, "You bring out the best in me. I love you too."

Caryn reached up to kiss his lips and then wrapped her arms around him and they fell asleep.

BREAKFAST

Kimberly usually woke up after Will left for work, but last night they had a huge fight and she didn't sleep well. She and Will stayed on their sides of the bed as if there was a wall between them. And Kim guessed there was. She and Will were at an impasse about him taking a weekend trip with his friends, without her. One of Will's college friends had tickets to the All-Star game in New York. It was suppose to be a guy's weekend. Kim couldn't understand why she couldn't at least spend the weekend with him. This was their first major fight as a married couple and the first time they didn't make love since they had gotten married seven months ago. Of course they had disagreements over minor issues and had to adjust to growing pains of living together, but this was their first real fight.

Kim knew the advice she and Will had gotten about never going to bed angry with each other made sense. It seemed the more they talked the worse things got until Kim went to bed without settling anything, and angry with her husband. And so now it was morning as she lay next to her husband and she didn't know how to bridge the gap.

As she lay in bed contemplating her dilemma, Kim felt her stomach growl and so she decided to get up and make breakfast. She thought she would make Will's favorite and that would help say, "Honey, can we talk.' He loved hash browns, eggs, sausage and pancakes drowned in maple syrup, but ate them rarely while trying to maintain a health conscious diet. Kim decided to give him the works. So armed with a plan to open the communication she quietly headed for the kitchen.

As she cooked, Kim had an idea. She would fix him breakfast as well as seduce him. Nothing better than a full stomach and hot sex in the morning. Besides, morning was one of their favorite times to make love. She loved when he rolled over on top of her still warm from sleep with his dick hard and ready to enter her. She was getting wet just thinking about it.

Now that she had a plan she needed to think of her approach. She wanted to do something special and different. She wanted to remind him of how much she loved him and that together they would weather the storms of being newlyweds. Kim finished cooking breakfast and then she ran to shower before Will woke up. She was surprised that he didn't wake up with the smell of the food.

What Kim didn't know was that Will was lying in bed trying to think of a way to make up to his wife. He knew that he wasn't just trying to get Kim to see his point of view. He was trying to make her see that he was right, and she was wrong, which really just made him wrong.

He could smell breakfast and hoped she wasn't so mad at him that she didn't cook anything for him. It smelled like his favorite. Will thought that this might be a sign that she wanted to make up. He heard the shower and thought that maybe he could join her and they could make up for last night with this morning. Will was getting hard with thoughts of his wife in the shower with water running over her body. He wanted to run his tongue everywhere that the water ran. He could imagine entering her wet pussy from behind while the hot water hit his back. He was getting so aroused that he was brick hard.

Before he could get up and make his thoughts a reality, the shower stopped. Will got up to take his own shower and joined Kim in the bathroom as she was toweling off.

She was bent over drying off her legs and Will looked at her body and was getting even more aroused if that was possible. He wasn't sure what to say after last night's fight. "Mornin' babe", he said as his eyes followed her movements. She looked up at him and smiled, "Morning." Will felt confident after her smile and reached forward to caress her hips. Her brown skin was as soft as silk. His hands slid between her thighs to the still damp curly hairs that covered the opening to her pussy. Kim moaned a soft sigh and stood straight. She stepped back to nestle her butt to his groin. She gyrated her hips against his dick and knew he was ready for more. Kim turned around in his arms to face him, "Why don't you take a shower and I'll finish breakfast." Will was only thinking about tasting his wife, not breakfast. He lowered his head and began suckling her erect nipples. Will knew that she loved to have her breast licked.

Will was surprised when Kim pulled away with a groan. He could always be sure that there was more to come if he gave her nipples special attention. Kim said, "Baby, why don't you shower. I have a surprise waiting for you in the kitchen." Will responded with, "Hey, I have your surprise right here." as he stroked his stiff rod. Kim chuckled as she stepped away, "Later big boy. Just take your shower and join me in the kitchen."

Will jumped in the shower with thoughts of making up with his wife. The warm water running off the tip of his dick made him think of her tongue licking him. He could barely rinse off without thoughts of Kim sliding against his wet body. He hoped she was as aroused as he was, because that always led to great sex for the both of them.

Kim went to the kitchen with thoughts of things to come. Hopefully, multiple cums for the both of them. She remained nude under a short robe after scenting her body with one of her favorite perfumes. She arranged the food on the table so that they could feed each other with their fingers. Everything was in bite size pieces. There were no serving or eating utensils. Kim was trying to hurry so that she could be ready before Will got out of the shower. She was already very aroused after playing with him in the bathroom. If it wouldn't have spoiled her plans, she would have joined him in the shower. She could feel her juices between her thighs as she thought of what she was going to do with her husband.

Kim heard the shower stop; she dropped her robe and walked across the room naked. All the food was in place on the table as Kim sat down. She held the newspaper in front of herself and pretended to read. She didn't want Will to know she was naked until she could show him.

Will came into the kitchen hoping to serve his wife something along with her breakfast. He was surprised to see her reading the paper, something she never did. As he got closer to her he noticed her bare shoulders. He was so distracted by Kim's change in behavior and her promise for something special for him in the kitchen that he barely noticed the food on the table. The scent did reach the hungry part of his brain because his stomach growled. Kim looked up at him over the paper and said, "Hi honey. Why don't you join me and we can eat?" Will pulled out a chair opposite Kim's and sat down. His mouth dropped open when Kim put the paper aside and Will saw that she sat before him naked. Her bare breast faced him with her nipples erect and at attention as if calling to him. The morning light danced along the brown skin on her shoulders.

As Kim smiled, Will's manhood rose to attention under his robe. He had come to the table in just his robe in hopes of making love to his wife, but had no idea she was waiting for him like this. His hunger for food forgotten, Will stood up opened his robe and presented his wife with evidence of his hunger for her. Kim had to drag her eyes from the delectable site before her. She wanted to make this last and enjoy the meal she had planned for the two of them. "Why don't you sit down and let me get you something to eat", she said. "That may be hard to do in my present condition. Why don't we do something about this first and then we can feast?" Will said as he stroked his stiff dick. Kim chuckled and said, "If you can wait then, there is more for you to sample." and put a sausage between her lips and sucked.

Will's brain was deprived of oxygen because all of the blood in his body was pooling in his groin. He couldn't think of what to do as he watched Kim's lips work back and forth on a sausage. He wanted to touch her, but then he didn't want to interrupt her show. He stepped back and collided with his chair and dropped in his seat. He knew how well she knew how to use her lips to give him pleasure, and found himself jealous of a sausage. He wanted any part of his body to be in her mouth.

Kim was getting so hot watching her husband get aroused. She had to stay focused to see this through. She just wanted to make love to her man, but she did want to add something new to the game. Kim bit into her sausage and heard Will moan. As she finished chewing she started pouring syrup over the pancakes. Will reached forward and stroked the side of her breast down to her nipple and then he squeezed her aching hard nipple. The sensation sent a jolt of pleasure to her center. Kim closed her eyes and let out a sigh of pleasure. Kim didn't notice the syrup now being poured on the floor.

Kim opened her eyes and looked at her husband through a desire filled haze. She felt something wet at her feet and looked down in time to see the mess she had made with the syrup. "Oh no! Look what I've done. Man, you've got my head spinning so that I poured syrup on the floor." Kim said as she looked down at the floor. Will just grinned. It gave his male ego a boost to know that he had it like that with his wife.

"Let me get something to clean up this mess." Kim said as she started toward the sink for a towel. Will watched his wife's rear end as she sauntered across the room. It aroused him even more to watch her walk and to see the movement of her hips as they swayed and her thighs as they glided. To see her bare back made him want to rub her down from head to toe with a sensual massage.

Kim came back to the table and bent to the floor and began wiping up the syrup. As she wiped, she noticed that she was in the perfect spot to give Will head. Just the idea of licking him made her mouth water. Kim then thought that a little syrup might change the flavor and make it sweeter, for them both.

The sight of her backside in the air entranced Will. Thoughts of entering her vagina from behind crowded his mind. The image of sliding in and out of her wetness made his heart race. Will was so into his visual images that he was startled by the cool wet sensation that was applied to his balls. He next felt a wet and warm feeling and then felt the head of his dick enter Kim's mouth. "Baby...Oh Baby. What are you doing Baby? Oh baby that feels so good. What...Mmmm." Will felt Kim licking his balls and sucking his dick. Kim worked her hand up and down his shaft creating an erotic tension in him that he knew was going to explode. Kim started rubbing him in that special spot he liked, right under his testicles, before his anus. Just the right amount of pressure was enough to give him an explosive orgasm.

Will didn't want to cum yet. He wanted to be inside of Kim when he came. Will looked down under the table and reached for Kim. When he saw her kneeling at his groin he almost filled her mouth with his cum. Just to see her doing him with such love and attention was a powerful sight. Will said, "Baby, come here. Let me give you some lovin, like you've been giving me. I want to make you squirm." Kim was enjoying his pleasure so much that she didn't want to stop. But her body was calling for her to let him please her. Kim's nipples were hard and she was so wet that her juices were running down her thighs. Her body heat was high and she was short of breath. She wanted to feel her man inside of her. Kim kissed the head of his penis and felt it tremble, and stood up from under the table. She stood in front of her husband waiting for him to make the next move. Her mind was so aroused that she couldn't move.

Will could tell that his baby was over stimulated. He knew he would have to do something to ease the erotic tension for the two of them. Will stood and picked Kim up in his arms. He wanted her so bad that he didn't think he could make it to the bedroom. He sat her on the counter and looked at the feast before him. The food on the table had no appeal to him with the woman of his dreams in his arms. Will took her breasts into his palms, lifting them to his mouth. He suckled from her nipples and began satiating his desire with her pleasure. Kim squirmed on the counter and spread her legs for him to nestle between them.

She could feel the body of his penis rest against her pubic hairs as if bowing and asking to enter. Kim slid closer to him to encourage his taking her, but Will shook his head no. "I want to make you feel good. I want you to wait a little longer. You have the best breast in the world. I want to enjoy them longer", said Will with his mouth still full of her voluptuous breast. Will replaced his mouth with his thumbs and stroked her nipples back and forth. He began kissing her lips and put his tongue in her mouth. Will insistence that they wait reminded Kim of when they were first dating and could kiss and touch each other all night. He wrapped his arms around her and pulled her to his body. Will inhaled the scent of her hair and skin and felt drunk with the power she gave him.

Will could wait no more and he positioned himself to enter his wife. Kim was so ready for him that she spread her thighs and moved towards him. At the moment of joining, they both moaned each other's name. They each would swear it had never felt so good until the next time. They moved back and forth with each other to bring each other to climax. The goal was to please the other and that added to the enjoyment for themselves. They were in sync with each other's movements and working their way toward satisfying each other.

Kim could feel her vagina tightening around his dick. Her heart was pounding and she was out breath. She was about to cum. She wanted to wait for Will. "Honey. Oh Honey! I'm about to cum. I want you to cum with me." Will could feel the pressure of his heightened excitement. He was getting hot and sweating from the work he was exerting to please his wife. He could feel himself filling up with his cum. He was about to explode.

They looked in each other's eyes and moved together to bring each other to their satisfaction. Kim couldn't hold back any longer. "Oh Will! Oh Will! Baby, you're making me feel so good. Will! Will! Oh Willlll." she said as she came. Will could barely hear her moans of pleasure as she came because he was there himself. "Oh Kim! Baby you do me so good. Kim I love you. I love you baby. Ohhhh!"

They fell into each other's arms out of breath and pleased. Their love glowed between them as they caressed each other's back. "So how was breakfast?" Kim asked as she kissed Will's lips. Will chuckled and looked at the table of untouched food, "Well, the appetizer was great, but if we're gonna have the main course it needs to be warmed up." Kim smiled at him and said, "Well I think I want some more appetizer in the bedroom, that is if you can handle it?" "Woman! Who do you think I am, that I can't handle my responsibilities? Of course I'm up to the requested menu."

With that decided, Will helped Kim off the countertop and they headed to the bedroom. "Now how about me having dinner waiting for you when you get back from All-Star Weekend?" "Well baby if dinner is any thing like breakfast, I'd rather stay home and have breakfast, lunch and dinner with you." Kim looked at Will and said, "Honey I love you, but you go on and enjoy your weekend with the guys and I'll be here waiting for you."

DINNER DATE

Stephanie and David had been invited to this dinner party over one month ago. It was the president of David's company and it was a sign that the promotion he had been working towards was getting closer to reality. It was a major feather in his cap that they were invited to this dinner party. And even knowing that, Stephanie did not want to go. She knew how much it meant to David and had every intention of acting the corporate wife, but she just wanted to stay home and make love to her husband instead of boring conversation with stuffy VIPs and their wives.

Stephanie was not the typical wife of an up-and-coming company man. She worked as a nurse at the county children's hospital and enjoyed her job. The days could be long and draining, but fulfilling. David told her she didn't have to work, but she couldn't see wasting the years of school she put in to get her degree. Besides she loved what she did. And that was one of the problems with mingling with the company wives. She had a career outside the home and they made their career out of their social obligations and charity work. It left them with little to talk about. Stephanie decided that tonight she was going to mention the hospital fund-raiser that she was co-chairperson of and try to drum up some support from their hostess and fellow guest.

David was in the shower and all Stephanie could think about as she put on her makeup was joining him and sliding her body against his. 'Girl, that kind of thinking isn't going to get you anywhere. David will not be persuaded with foreplay tonight.' But all Stephanie could think about was making love to her husband. He had gone on for days

24

about how things could change for him if he made a good impression with the company executives. Stephanie decided to wear the diamond earrings and solitaire diamond necklace David had given her as a fifth wedding anniversary gift. She sat at her vanity mirror and admired the reflection from the light of the gems on her skin. She remembered the night David gave them to her. He was standing behind her massaging her shoulders when she felt coolness at her throat. She reached up to feel the necklace as he clasped it behind her neck. Stephanie looked down and screamed with awe and joy at what she found. She turned in David's arms to kiss him when he presented her with the earrings. Stephanie was speechless as tears came to her eyes. That night she made love with her husband in her diamonds. David's eyes followed her around the room as she modeled for him in just her diamonds and the afterglow of making love.

Stephanie came back to the present and wondered if she could remind David of that night if she was wearing just her diamonds when he came out of the shower. Maybe then she could convince him to loosen up and arrive fashionably late. Stephanie then thought better of it and decided to not get herself too aroused with no relief soon in sight.

After finishing her hair Stephanie had an inspiring thought. She may not be able to convince David to arrive late, but she could entice him all night long. She decided to wear a garter belt and stockings and nothing else under her evening gown. At some point during the night she would let him know and then she tease him and remind him all night long. Maybe he will be so aroused that they will come home and make up for a boring dinner with dessert in bed. With that in mind Stephanie wanted to hurry and dress so that she could surprise David with her lack of lingerie later.

David came out of his dressing room in his tuxedo, just as Stephanie was putting on her favorite cologne at strategic places. "Baby, you look marvelous. Almost good enough to eat." David said as he admired his wife. Stephanie was dressed in a smoke gray silk, strapless evening dress. It hugged her in all the right places while leaving him wanting for more. She was wearing the diamonds he had given her. He remembered the night he gave them to her and the way she modeled for him in just the diamonds. He could still remember the sway of her stride and the smile on her lips. He could almost swear to still tasting her kisses. He knew he was a lucky man to have her as his wife. She was smart, gorgeous, loved him and had a sexual appetite always that left him satisfied.

Stephanie could tell she had David's attention. She raised the edge of her dress to adjust her stocking to her garter strap. She positioned herself so that David has full view of her thigh. She heard David take in a deep breath and knew she had put something on his mind. David cleared his throat and said, "Honey, are you about ready to go?" Stephanie said, "Sure. Let me just grab my purse and wrap." He said, "Take your time I'll go pull the car around."

Stephanie met David at the front of their home. He saw her to the car and they headed to the home of the company's president, Mr. McKnight. "Honey, How long do you think we will have to stay to fulfill your duty at this dinner?" Stephanie asked as she adjusted her dress and showed a little thigh. David took his eyes off the road momentarily to look at Stephanie. He barely noticed the length of her dress and said, "Babe, you know how important this is to me and how important it is that I come across well. We can't just eat and run." "I know, but tell me we aren't gonna be the last ones to leave." He said, "I can't promise you that, but I'll try and keep it as short as possible." Stephanie looked at David and said, "Well I want to get home early enough to show you what I'm not wearing under my dress."

David looked at Stephanie and said, "What do you mean?" Stephanie told him, "I don't have on anything between me and my dress. Or should I say I'm only wearing my diamonds and my dress." and raised the edge of dress even further to show him her garter. They were lucky there was no oncoming traffic. David could barely keep his eyes on the road. "Honey, watch where you're driving. You don't want to hit anyone." David asked Stephanie, "Why aren't you wearing anything under that dress?" She said," I wanted to give you something to want to rush home for."

David pulled into the driveway of the home of Mr. and Mrs. Kevin McKnight. He handed the keys to the valet and escorted his wife to the door. Stephanie knew David was distracted and probably wasn't clear as to what possessed her to pull such a stunt. But if he thought back to their days of courtship, then he would remember that they always surprised each other. She feared she was in danger of him turning into a boring company man and wanted her to be the stuffy company man's wife. She had to spice things up. Their intimate moments were wonderful, but a little spice was always nice.

David and Stephanie were met at the door by the butler who showed them in. Mr. and Mrs. McKnight were in the entrance foyer greeting their guests. The house was at it's finest. There was the air of elegance everywhere around them. As Stephanie and David approached their hosts, Mr. McKnight said, "David, good to see you. Is this your lovely wife? No wonder you rush home every night." Mrs. McKnight nudged her husband in his side for what she thought was an inappropriate comment. "Kevin, leave the man alone. You want him to feel welcome in our home, don't you?" Mrs. McKnight turned to Stephanie and said, "Forgive my husband's lack of social grace. I am Nancy McKnight. Believe me I've been married to the man for 30 years and his bark is worse than his bite. He has to make his employees think he's a tough guy, but he's a kitten at home." Mr. McKnight coughed loudly as if to drown out his wife's word. "Honey, let this couple join in the festivities. We will have the chance to chat with them later. David, my good fellow, enjoy! You and your beautiful wife, enjoy!"

David escorted Stephanie into the ballroom that had been decorated to accentuate the high windows and ceiling. There were tables with magnificent floral centerpieces and a dance floor. David said to Stephanie, "You see what I mean? He's watching me and I have to put my best foot forward. Did you hear him say that's why he sees me rushing home? He's watching me." Stephanie looked at David and said, "Man, would you cool out?! He's just trying to intimidate you. That's his job in order to get the most work out of you. You know how good you are at your job, and you would not have come as far as you did if you weren't as good as you are. The department heads of your other positions thought you were good enough to promote. So stop worrying and let's enjoy. The champagne that is flowing around here must be some of the best. Let's mingle and have some." David looked at his wife. He loved her undying support of him. With her in his corner he could always make it. Besides, she's right. His prior work speaks for itself and he know he's good at his job. If he could just convince the right people of that.

Stephanie and David had a glass of champagne and found their table. They were seated with some of the people David would work with if he got his promotion. David said to Stephanie, "Great! I get to be interviewed across the banquet table." Stephanie asked what he meant by that and he told her whom they were dining with. Stephanie had enough. She made up her mind to seduce her husband and take his mind off of the stresses of work and his possible promotion.

Stephanie sat closer to her husband and placed her hand on his thigh under the table. She enjoyed the strength she felt at her fingertips and moved her hand over his thigh, enjoying the feel of the fabric sliding across his skin and his firm muscles tense and she continued her travels. She dipped her hand into his crotch and heard him take in a breath of air and cough as he tried to cover for the gap in conversation. Stephanie sat by his side smiling as if interested in every word of the conversation at the table. In actuality she had thoughts of other ways to taunt her husband slowly over the next few hours.

David leaned to Stephanie and whispered in her ear, "What are you doing?! What has gotten into you?!" Stephanie looked at him innocently and said, "Whatever are you speaking of?" "You know what I mean. Why are you so horny tonight?" Stephanie said, "Baby, you bring this out in me. I've been aching to get you in my stuff all night. If we had time I was going to join you in the shower. That's why I'm not wearing any underwear. If I get the chance I want you to have quick easy access to this hot wet spot between my thighs."

Stephanie could feel David's pants tighten at his crotch as his dick got brick hard. David moaned under his breath. "Girl, you know I adore you. I have been too distracted by things at work, but we've got to mix and mingle. I want to make a good impression. I'll tighten you up when we get home." The band started to play and Stephanie said, "That may not be soon enough." She grabbed his hand and said, "Let's dance. They're playing our song." David slowly stood up and said, "Slow down. I can hardly walk because my dick is so stiff. How am I suppose to dance so close to you and not come?" Stephanie had a mischievous look in her eyes and told him, "You tell me."

They took to the dance floor arm in arm. It was a slow song that called for close contact. It was just what Stephanie wanted and just what David dreaded in his current state. Stephanie pressed up against his erection and he moaned. David didn't know how long he was going to last this close to her as sexy as she looked and knowing she had on no lingerie. If she wasn't careful he was going to take her in a corner and have his way with her.

Little did David know that Stephanie was getting more aroused by the pressure of his dick against her belly. Her nipples were pressing on the fabric of her gown and the lapels of David's dinner coat were rubbing against them. She was creaming and just knew it was going to run down her legs. She wished she could reach down and hold his cock in her hands. She knew David would flip out if she did anything so openly bold, but she was going to have to do something soon.

The song ended and everyone applauded the band. Stephanie and David seemed to snap out of a trance. David's mouth was dry and he was in need of something cold on or in his body to cool the fire Stephanie had started.

The rush of desire to her sensual core dazed Stephanie. David escorted her to their table and went to the bar for drinks for the two of them. He returned to the table with her rum and Coke and his cognac. He knew he should abstain to keep his wits about himself, but champagne was not enough tonight.

The drink only seemed to make Stephanie hotter. She sat at the table appearing immersed in the various conversations, but her thoughts were really on devouring her husband. David responded to the questions by his dinner companions, but all he could think of was sinking into his wife's wetness.

After enduring an eight-course meal, David suggested that he and Stephanie take a walk in the courtyard. It was a warm night with the sky illuminated by a full moon. The flowers scented the evening air and acted as an aphrodisiac. David walked with Stephanie in his arms along a path that lead to a large tree that protected them from the view from the house. He swung Stephanie into his arms and devoured her lips. He seemed to drink from the passion in her body. His tongue played with hers and he took nibbles from her lips down to her neck. Stephanie's arousal was spinning out of control. David took the edge of her gown and raised it to feel her nakedness. They moaned simultaneously as he found her clit. She was wet and ready. He dipped his finger in and out of her juices and used them to his travels into her vagina.

Stephanie pressed into his hand. She wanted more. She wanted his hard dick in her wetness. Her nipple strained against the fabric of her gown. David took his other hand and caressed the swell of her ass and pulled her into him. Stephanie reached for his trousers and found his zipper. She released him from their confinement. She was surprised to find he was bare. David chuckled and said, "You're not the only one with something up their sleeve, or should I say nothing." Stephanie smiled and said, "And here I was thinking you were getting stuffy and too corporate minded. Baby, can we get out of here now?" David said, "Yes, before we end up on the ground in the garden. We surely couldn't return to the table with grass stains on our evening clothes. But let's hope we don't run into anyone like the McKnight's."

David helped Stephanie rearrange her dress and she zipped his pants and they headed back to the party. After they had Stephanie's wrap they turned to leave and bumped right into the McKnight's. Mr. McKnight said, "David, you aren't leaving so soon?" with a look of disapproval. David stuttered and said, "Well, um yes we are. David and I have some early morning plans." David prayed they didn't smell the scent of Stephanie's juices. David was in his arms and all he could think of was sinking into her. Mrs. McKnight said, "Leave them alone. Don't you remember what it was like to be young and in love?" She smiled at Stephanie and Stephanie returned the smile from David's arms.

David and Stephanie said their good nights and waited for their car. David seemed to have lost some of his passion. He said, "I hope I don't get demoted instead of promoted." Stephanie looked at him and said, "Let's not go through that again. If you aren't good enough for them then you will find another company that is better for you. Now let's go home and let me model my diamonds for you."

They got home and made love until the early morning. David got up and decided to go into the office for a couple of hours as Stephanie slept. When David got to the office, he ran into Mr. McKnight in the elevator. Mr. McKnight saw David and said, "Well, I'm surprised to see you here. I thought you had early plans today?" David said, "Stephanie is sleeping in and so I thought I'd come and check on a few things." "Well, I was going to wait to see you on Monday, but I'd guess sooner is better than later. Why don't you meet me in my office in fifteen minutes." "Sure Mr. McKnight." David said as he watched Mr. McKnight leave the elevator at his floor. He just knew this was it. He might as well start packing his desk up. His heart pounded in his chest as he went to his office. David sat to compose his thoughts before going to see the boss.

Fifteen minutes later he knocked at Mr. McKnight's door. "Come in and have a seat. "David thought he would rather stand for the bad news, but decided not to challenge Mr. McKnight. "David, you have been with this company for five years and your work record is outstanding. We have been watching you to move you up when Mr. Davis retired. But as you know he has decided to stay and help open our new offices in Chicago. I was going to wait to tell you this, but I guess now is as good as time as any. We are going to have you go to Chicago to take over that office when Mr. Davis leaves." David was speechless. He wasn't sure he heard Mr. McKnight correctly. He just knew he was being fired or sent back down the corporate ladder a few rungs. "Well, what do you say? Are you interested? Do you think your wife will be willing to move?" David's head was spinning. He had to rethink his plans. He was going to be packing his desk up, but for a move to Chicago! "Mr. McKnight, I am honored by your offer. I will have to discuss this with Stephanie, but I am sure she will be as excited as I am."

Mr. McKnight said, "I did have my doubts about your dedication to the company, but my wife said that if your dedication to the company was half of your dedication to your wife then we had to consider you. I always take my wife's advice. After you left last night, she couldn't stop talking about the sparkle in the your eyes'. Last night she even got a little frisky just thinking about the passion that surrounded the two of you."

David said, "Thank you, Mr. McKnight. If you don't mind, I want to go home and tell my wife the news. I also always take her advice. I thank you, again and will see you Monday."

David ran to the elevator, to his car and sped home. He climbed in bed with his wife and cuddled up to her bare behind. Stephanie snuggled back into him and said, "I thought you were going in to the office?" David kissed her shoulders and said, "I did. I ran into Mr. McKnight and he offered me a promotion...in Chicago." Stephanie screamed and sat up in bed. Her bare breast catching David's eyes. "How can you come in here so calmly and whisper that? Honey, that's wonderful! I told you everything was going to work out just fine." David reached forward and played with her nipples. Stephanie moaned her pleasure and reached for David. They tumbled together and spent the morning in bed celebrating their love and David's promotion

DREAMIN'

Dear Lover,

It is 3:00 a.m. and I just woke up from the most erotic dream about you. I feel like I just came and that you must have been here with me. My knees are weak and my nipples are hard. My pubic hairs are wet from the juices that my dreams of you have produced. My breath is short and shallow and I can almost smell your scent next to me. I had to wake up and tell you how you made me feel.

It has been so long since you have laid between my thighs that I ache for your return. I want to feel your hard dick fill me. I want to feel your come coat the walls of my pussy and feel you drive into me as you reach your point of no return. My nipples are hard and straining for some sort of contact. Just the weight of my shirt against my bare breasts is making me wet. I can just imagine your tongue licking my nipples and your lips suckling my breasts. I can feel the heat between my thighs as you scrape your teeth across my nipples. I want to call you and ask you to come over and help me relieve the heaviness between my thighs, but since I cannot, I must share my dream with you...

I don't know how I got there. I'm not aware of the time of day or night. My first memory is of kissing someone. Their lips are familiar. The taste and feel are making me hot. I feel like I want to breathe in every breath he breathes out. I know that I love him and I feel very safe and secure in his arms. I'm afraid to open my eyes for the fear that he will disappear. My body tells me that it's been a long time since I've made love. I am light-headed as if all the blood in my brain has rushed to my cunt. It feels hot

35

as the pressure builds between my thighs. My hands are on his shoulders. I recognize these shoulders and arms. His hands are on my thighs. His hands are moving back and forth creating heat. They act as if they want to go further, but don't know where to go. My hands move down his arms to his hands. I know his hands. I can feel the finger he broke playing high school football. I know his large, strong, skillful hands.

I want to open my eyes, but they feel so heavy. My eyelids flutter and I see that it's you. I open my eyes completely and we make contact. I am so happy to see you that my heart feel like it's going to burst from the joy and love you make me feel. I look around without our lips ever separating and realize that we are in the back seat of a cab. The seat is old, cracked, burgundy leather with tape holding together the edges behind our knees. I smell the faint scent of strawberry pimp oil and your cologne. It's your scent that fills my head and lungs. I hope it is on my skin after you leave so I can go home, smell you on my body and remember the passion.

I don't know who is driving or if we are even moving, but we are together. It almost seems as if the seat we are sitting on is a prop from a stage play. There is no front, sides or rear to the car, just the floor, our seat and each other. My legs are bare and your hands are caressing them. As your hands go up and between my thighs it is revealed to us that I am not wearing panties. We both seem surprised. I spread my legs further apart to give you room to feel how pleased I am to have you there. Your fingers travel across my mound of hair and I feel my heart racing. I realize that I am just sitting there. I need to touch you. I need to feel you erect penis in my hands to feel validated, to feel that you want me. I move my hands to your groin and find what I desire, a big hard dick. As I touch it, you move closer to me. I can feel you fingers moving, separating the wet lips that reveal my womanhood. You touch inside of me and then smooth the wetness across my clit. A moan escapes my lips as you slide your finger back and forth across my sensitive, swollen nub of flesh.

I feel as if I am going to pass out with the building urgency I am feeling. I want to touch you. My fingers frantically release the belt at your waist. I release the button of your pants and unzip the zipper. You aren't wearing underwear. I am granted immediate access to your cock. We slide your pants down your legs to pool at your feet. Your dick almost seems to leap in my hands as I caress it. Just holding you in my hands is making my mouth water with the desire to taste you. I rub my thumb across the tip of your dick and there is a drop of your wetness ready for my tongue. I lick my thumb to taste your flavor. Your eyes follow my every movement. I sit back in the seat so that I can lean forward enough to take you in my mouth comfortably. My mouth is watering. I must swallow before I can open my mouth because I just might drool and you would see how hungry I am for you. I lean forward and take the tip of your penis in my mouth. My tongue swirls around its head and my mind is racing. I can't decide if I should take you in my mouth to the base of your penis or if I should lick you up and down with my tongue. I am firmly holding the base of your penis in one hand while the other holds your balls. I stroke you up and down with my mouth. I can feel the muscles tighten in your thighs. You reposition yourself so that I can stroke you more comfortably. I feel your penis get harder and I want your to release to come soon. You move your penis from

Chrystine Dier

my mouth and say you want to touch me. I am so wet that there is a puddle where I sit.

You lay me down and my back makes contact with a soft surface. I look around and realize that I am now in a bed. It is a canopy bed with sheer white curtains draped from the top of the canopy to enclose us. We are lying on satin sheets. There are candles lit around the room casting a romantic glow.

You unbutton my blouse to reveal my bare breast. I slide my skirt over my hips with your help. You are kneeling between my thighs. My legs are open and my knees are slightly bent. You gently pull at my pubic hairs and this produces an unusually pleasurable sensation. My arms are outstretched and my hands grab the sheets. You spread my labia and slide two fingers into my waiting vagina. The feeling is so good that I raise my hips off the bed to allow your fingers to go deeper. You start moving your fingers in and out. My hips are moving in rhythm with your fingers. Your eyes are watching me and I feel as if I can't control the movements of my own body. I feel as if someone is pulling a string that connects my nipples and vagina. As you continue to make love to me, it is getting tighter and more taut.

You rub your finger across my clit and remove the others from my vagina. I beg you not to stop. You lean over me to lick my nipple and then go to the other. You trail your kisses to my shoulder and neck, and then passionately kiss my lips. You take my breath away. You lay on top of me pressing your hard dick into my abdomen. My pelvis rocks against you hoping that this is the moment of truth. I spread my legs even further and wrap them around your waist. My arms encircle your back and I can feel your rippling muscles that are tense from you

38

supporting your weight on your hands. I run my hands down your back to your ass. It's as if I am trying to push your body into mine and make us become one.

You lift your mouth from mine and kiss my neck, my shoulders, and each nipple. You run your tongue between my breasts, down my belly to my navel, and then stop where my hair begins. I'm holding my breath hoping I know where you are going next. You seem to hesitate. I don't know if you are unsure or you are just torturing me. The wait is unbearable, but the anticipation is exciting. Your mouth goes lower to the opening to my womaness. Your tongue presses against my clit. Your tongue becomes stiff as if it were a small penis searching for the opening to my pleasure, and then it becomes soft and roams lower. It feels so good that my mind is spinning and my heart is pounding. I realize that I have forgotten to breathe. As I remember to take in a breath, I hear a sound and realize that it has come from me. I can hear myself moaning and calling your name. If I weren't so aroused I might be embarrassed, but right now I have to say your name just to remember to breathe. You tongue is moving up and down and back and forth. I feel like I want more. I need to feel you inside of me. I need to feel the fullness of your penis inside of my cunt. I'm desperate for the friction of you moving in and out of me.

As I lay there begging you to take me, I feel the pressure of what I think is your cock. I get excited and push my hips toward you. I realize that what I feel enter me is not your dick because it is vibrating. I ask you what you are doing and you tell me to just lay back and enjoy. At first it startles me, but then the feeling starts to get to me and I am enjoying the vibrations. You start moving the vibrator back and forth. I just know I am about to come.

Just when I think I can take no more, you put your mouth on me and lick my clit with your tongue.

My eyes are closed and my nipples are erect. Just the air on them is arousing. I feel the juices in my pussy flowing. "I'm coming! Oh baby, I'm coming!" You encourage me to come. You say, "That's it, come, baby." You rest the vibrator against my clit and add an extra spasm to my orgasm. My head is spinning. My ears are ringing. My arms and legs are weak. I'm trying to gather my senses because I want and need to make you come.

I reach forward to grasp your dick. You are rock hard like a teenage boy about to make love for the very first time. You look me in the eye as if begging me to help you. I stroke your penis back and forth with my hands. I reach up to kiss you passionately and express my desire for you. Even though you gave me a wonderful orgasm, I still need to feel you inside of me. I pull you down to me and guide you into my wet cunt. I have the feeling of coming home to a comfortable, favorite pair of slippers. As we start to move in and out, the feeling of comfort is replaced by a feeling of urgency. I feel that if we stop I will die. I am out of breath and I can hear you saying my name in my ear. You kiss me passionately and I feel myself about to come. I try to wait for you so that we can come together. I feel you increase the pace the way you do when you are almost there. I keep up with you to help you go over the edge and just when I don't think I can go any longer, I feel the spasm of your orgasm. My own release is seconds behind yours. You collapse on top of me, out of breath. My heart fills with joy from having you with me. You rise to look me in my eyes to say, "I love you." Just those three simple words brings tears to my eyes and I say, "I love you too". We fall asleep with thoughts of making love in a few hours after we rest.

The next time I wake up, I am at home and all alone. I can't tell if what I have experienced was a dream or reality. My body feels as if it is ready for you. I feel wetness on my face as if I have been crying. And this is when I realize that it was a dream. Instantly I feel lonely. I want desperately to call you and share my thoughts with you, but all I can do is write it down to share it with you when we next meet.

HER FAVORITE THING

If there was one things Lynette could say she loved without reason was her man's dick. She loved him more than mere words could express, but her lust of his dick was even more difficult to explain.

She loved everything about it and just thinking about it heightened her lustful longings for it. Some days she could barely make it until it was time to go home because of thoughts of what she craved to do to it and with it. She could be at work and become so aroused by fantasies of touching it, holding it, arousing it, and tasting it, that she had to discreetly go to the ladies room and masturbate to relieve some of the tension.

Lynette came home one evening after a particularly stimulating day of craving Arthur dick. All she wanted to do was lay her man down and love him from head to toe with a prolonged detour in the middle. She hurriedly slipped into something more comfortable. Just the weight of her breast as they were released from her bra was arousing. The fabric of her negligee rubbing against her nipples felt like torture. She was being turned on and Arthur wasn't there yet to do anything about it.

When she heard his key in the door she started his shower and then met him at the front door. She took his briefcase and placed it on the floor and slipped into his arms. Arthur smiled and said, "Oh, I know what this is about. I hear the shower and you're meeting me at the front door rubbing yourself against me." Lynette looked up as she pressed her pelvis into his groin and said, "Okay, so you know what this is about, but you can't tell me you don't like it."

Lynette reached between them for his dick and felt the imprint of it as it begin to harden in her hand. As she stroked him he moaned her name, "Oh Lynette. Girl, you know what you do to me. Let me take my shower and I'll meet you in the bedroom." Arthur pulled away and walked to the bedroom to undress.

Lynette went to the bedroom after she heard him in the shower. She picked up the clothes he had left on the floor in his haste to get undressed. She smelled the remnants of his cologne in his clothes and her heart started to beat faster. She loved the way he smelled. She lay down across the bed and day dreamed about sucking his dick. She loved everything about that part of his body. She thought God had out done himself when he created the human male's penis. She often wondered if she suffered from penis envy. But then she thought not, because if she had her own then she wouldn't be able to enjoy it as much as she did Arthur's. As she pondered those thoughts, she heard the shower stop and knew he would be joining her soon. She felt like a kid waiting for Christmas.

Arthur came into the bedroom with a towel around his waist. Lynette couldn't wait to unwrap her present. Arthur had that gleam in his eyes that told her it was going to be a passion filled evening. Lynette knew he liked to see her naked, but she didn't want him to have any distractions. Tonight was her night to have fun.

Arthur stopped at the edge of the bed and said to her, "Why don't you take that off and let me cuddle up next to you?" She said, "No. You know if I do where things will end up. Why don't you drop the towel and come here?" Arthur did just that and crawled to Lynette and kissed her lips as if sucking the sweetness out of a piece of fruit. Lynette felt her arousal curling up from the core of her female essence, like tendrils of smoke dissipating into the air. Her nipples hardened as Arthur reached forward to stroke her breast.

Lynette stopped his hand; her voice deepened from arousal, "No baby. I want to taste you. I've been wanting this all day. Let me suck you." Lynette rolled him to his back, lay across him with her breast on his chest and began kissing his lips. She placed tiny whispers of kisses along his neck to his chest as she moved down his body. She stopped at his nipples to circle them each with her tongue. She continued down his abdomen with more kisses. Lynette looked to her left to his awaiting penis and looked at its erectness, likening it to a solider at attention. When she got to his navel she dipped her tongue in and out. She saw Arthur's thigh muscles tighten. It was always a part of the game for Arthur to fight to remain in control and for Lynette to try to break his will. Lynette could see him flexing his toes and heard the stirrings of a moan in his chest.

Lynette continued on her path from his navel to the line that started his pubic hairs. She parted his pubic hairs with her tongue until she got to the base of his penis. Arthur was fully erect and Lynette was ready to take as much of him into her mouth as her tongue and throat would allow. She held his dick up straight and slid her tongue from base to tip. It was as if his penis had a mind of it's own. She felt it move in her hands. Arthur was grabbing the sheets on either side of himself and balling them in his fists.

As Lynette took the head of his penis into her mouth, Arthur raised his hips as if hurrying the moment. Lynette took her mouth away form his dick and said, "Baby, I am running this show. Now you just lay there and let me have my fun." Arthur said in a deeply aroused voice, "Baby, you know I can't help myself when you're doing me like this. You're just to fucking good at it." Lynette loved hearing him tell her how good she was at giving him pleasure. He didn't know how much pleasure it gave her to be doing him.

Lynette returned to the head of his penis and wrapped her lips around it. She slid her tongue around that rim and then ran her tongue across the slit at the top. As she sucked the head she took in sips of air between sucks. The coldness always took Arthur by surprise and aroused him. She took a little more of him into her mouth and the sucked her way back to the head. She went down a little further and then repeated that same action. She pulsed up and down on the head of his penis like a quickie, fast short pumps. She continued that and each time taking in more and more of his rock hard cock until she was almost to the base. Arthur was squirming. He was trying to maintain his control. He knew if he could hold on, it would be even more explosive when he came.

He loved looking down and watching Lynette's head bobbing up and down as she took him into her mouth. She was so good at giving him pleasure. Arthur believed that the fact that she loved it so much made it more enjoyable for them both. Some women had to be asked or begged to give their man head. Lynette enjoyed it from the moment it was introduced to their lovemaking. Arthur also loved going down on her, but that was another story. The fact that they shared a passion for oral sex and each other always made for exciting lovemaking. The feeling Lynette was generating in his body interrupted Arthur's thoughts. He was about to come and found himself unable to control his movements. He was raising his ass off the bed, meeting her stroke for stroke.

Lynette knew she had him when he started fucking her mouth. She was so aroused that she was wet and about to come herself. Just watching him loose control was a sexy sight, and to know she was causing it. She increased her pace and stroked him with one hand as she concentrated her mouth on the head of his penis. She had her other hand caressing his balls and occasionally stroking the spot before his asshole with her finger. She tasted his pre come on her tongue and knew he was going to come soon. She could feel his penis swell in her hand as it does before he comes.

Lynette was so into her rhythm that she was taken by surprise when Arthur turned her over on her back. Lynette looked at Arthur and said, "What the hell are you doing! Arthur! Arthur?" Arthur wasn't hearing her because he was in the zone of sexual haze. He wanted to come in Lynette's pussy, not her mouth. The thought came between moments of pleasure to take control of this situation. He looked in her eyes as he slid his full dick into her sweet, wet pussy, "Baby, I know it's what you like to do and control is part of it for you, but I want to come inside you. Just let me make you feel good. You know you want it, you know I can feel how wet you are." Arthur slid his dick in and out and took Lynette to a place of intense pleasure. Just as she thought she couldn't take much more she felt the inner coil that was tightening inside of her explode. "Arthur. Oh baby. Mmmmm. And Arthur was on his own trip of pleasure as he called her name as he exploded.

Arthur lay on top of Lynette out of breath and energy and thinking, 'That was intense.' As much as he loved to let her suck him off, he loved stroking her pussy even more. Lynette lay there stunned by Arthur's taking over and it made her hot just thinking about it. That was

46

something different for him to stop and fuck her. He was so ready that he just took it as well as giving it to her.

They lay in each other's arms and drifted to sleep to rejuvenate themselves for round two. They both thought as they drifted off about how much they loved each other and how they enjoyed their ever changing an always exciting sex life.

Chrystine Dier

<u>GIVING</u>

Ahhhh! I was finally here. Home. All I could think about today was coming home to be with my man. My thoughts were interrupted as I tried to concentrate during a meeting with my boss. At lunch I had to retreat to the ladies room and relieve some tension by rubbing my clit. On the train ride home each vibration of my seat heightened my arousal. Even as I took a leisurely soak in the tub, the water moving against my sensitive nipples excited me. I craved as a starving man would a meal.

All I could think about all day was lying in bed next to him as he slept and giving him head. I loved his dick. It was the most perfect one I had ever had the pleasure of knowing. I loved waking in the middle of the night and finding his resting, warm, manhood under the covers. I would caress it, enjoying the soft, silky textures. I could feel it responding to my attention, as if a separate being from the man.

I would continue giving it the attention that would make it as hard as I liked. I would duck my head under the covers to take him in my mouth. My mouth is watering in anticipation. I would slide the head into my partially opened mouth, moving my tongue around the head and following the ridge all the way around. I would slip the tip of my tongue over the opening at the top. As I tasted his precome I would know he was awaking to his aroused state. He would reach under the covers to rub my shoulders and neck. I hear him moan and shift his hips to a more comfortable position.

I take him fully into my mouth to its base. I slide my tongue up the underside, following that big, throbbing vein to the tip. I purse my lips to make a tight ring around his dick and work my mouth up and down. It seems to get harder and fuller. I alternate between sucking up and down and holding him firmly in my hand. My other hand is busy holding his balls and massaging that spot behind them, just the way he likes.

He starts to move his hips as if fucking my mouth. I am getting so turned on that I am creaming and am wet. As he moves, his thigh rubs against my nipple and adds to my aroused state. I don't want to stop until he comes and shoots his juices into my mouth. I want to make him call my name. I love to wake him from a sleep because all of his defenses are down and reserves are removed. He can't stop himself from rocking in time with the pace of my mouth.

I feel his dick get fuller and know he is about to come. I work faster and add extra firmness from my mouth and hand. He is moaning as grabs the back of my head to control the rhythm. He is calling my name. He makes one, two and then three strong surges into my mouth and then I feel the warmth of his come in my mouth, on my tongue. I swallow without a thought.

I come from under the covers and lay chest to chest with him. I kiss him and slip my tongue into his mouth he deepens the kiss, and reaches under the covers to slide his finger into my wet cunt. He then takes his turn under the covers and gives me my pleasure.

"Baby, I'm home! Where are you?" "I'm in the tub!" He comes into the bathroom as looks at my naked form in the water. I see his erection rise up in his pants. He smiles and say, "Do you want to come out of there and take a nap. You are all I've thought about all day." I smile and say,

"Sure. I know what you mean." I climb out of the tub and start to make my memories a reality.

THE KISS

It all started with a kiss. I can still feel his lips against mine. It was one of those kisses you dream about. One of those kisses that you wet your panties just remembering... one that could make you cum...one of those kisses that you wish could go on forever.

I had fallen asleep on the couch waiting for him to come over. There was a fire in the fireplace and candlelight lit the room. There was sparkling wine chilling and glasses for two. I wore a slinky, red satin negligee with spaghetti straps that crossed in the back and dipped almost low enough to see the curve of my ass.

I loved to rub myself through the satin and feel the texture as it slid across my skin. I loved it even more when my lover caressed me with his satin touch...the pressure of his touch from soft to strong...the stroke of his tongue as it moved across my lips, corner to corner and down my throat to the hollow of my cleavage...the silken slide of his dick in and out of my womaness, the core of what makes me wet...the strength in his arms as he holds me close.

I heard his key in the door and the lock as it turned. I stood to greet him with a smile on my face and feeling hot for his touch. He opened his arms and I went to him. His arms enveloped me and I could feel the cold air from the night in his coat seep into my skin. I shivered and my nipples grew taut. He removed his coat while still holding me in his arms. I then felt the warmth from his body heat as he held me.

He looked down at me as I looked up at him. He lowered his lips to mine and kissed them. I kissed him back and took in the essence of his scent. I breathed in his breath as he breathed out. I could feel his presence in my heart and soul. He ran his tongue along my bottom lip to the right. He kissed with quick short pecks along my jaw line to my chin. He slid his tongue down my neck to suck and give a love bite, leaving his mark to claim me as his. I held my head back enjoying him enjoying me. What a powerful feeling to have your man lavish your skin with so much attention.

I wanted to feel his skin next to mine. I pulled his shirt from his pants, unbuttoned it and pressed my breast to his chest. I put my hands on either side of his face and kissed him deeply while pressing myself against him. I stiffened my tongue and inserted it into his mouth. I pulsed it in and out as if fucking his mouth. He sucked my tongue as if he were sucking my clit. He would dart his tongue side to side across my tongue and then suck.

He massaged my shoulders and caressed up and down my arms. I placed my hands at his waistband and released the snap on his jeans. I unzipped them and slid my hands inside with my palms toward his belly. My fingertips grazed his pubic hairs. I felt the muscles of his abdomen tense. I knew he anticipated my going further. I deepened my assault of his mouth as I slid my hands deeper.

He reached up between us and found my nipples. I moaned as he took one between his fingertips and rolled it. My nipple hardened between his fingers. He lowered my straps off my shoulders. He took his mouth from mine and took my other nipple into his mouth. He sucked and nibbled and flicked my nipple with his tongue as he continued to roll the other one between his fingers.

My head dropped back and my breast rose. He suckled as he caressed and kissed. My hands moved further into his pants and found his fully erect penis lying to the side as if looking for a way out. The silky feel of it always aroused me and made me bolder in my approach. I caressed it as I pulled it from its confinement. I could feel it harden even more as if that were possible. I felt the silken skin and the veins in my hand and began to stroke him up and down. He moaned my name and I wanted more. I wanted to give him more and make him feel more.

My hips were grinding into him as if controlled by some other force. My gown slid to my hips and he moved it past the fullness of my thighs and let it pool at my feet. I stood before him nude, vulnerable and aroused. I pulled his shirt from his shoulders and moved his jeans over his round firm buttocks.

I knelt down to remove his pants and my face was at his manhood. It was such an irresistible sight that I kissed it softly to say hello. It jumped as he moaned, "Mmm, baby." I put my tongue to its opening and licked. I opened my mouth and took its head into my mouth to rest against my tongue, just the tip. And I ran my tongue around the rim of it. I could feel his hand on my shoulders. He held on to me for support while his pants lay at his feet, still wearing his shoes.

He stood me up, pulled me to him and held my head between his hands as he kissed me. His hardness pressed into my belly. He slid his shoes off with his feet and stepped out of his jeans. We stood before each other with our bodies connecting from head to toe. I could feel his heartbeat tapping out a rhythm with mine.

I wanted him between my thighs. I wanted him in me, on me, over me. He took his hand and slid it between my thighs. He used his finger to find my slit and separated my hairs to go deeper. He found my juices flowing and used them to lubricate and work my clit. I could feel a tightening in my gut. My breath was coming in short puffs. I could hear thunder in my ears as my blood roared through my body. I arched my back and tried to pull him closer to me. I wanted to straddle his arm. He was working me up to an orgasm that was draining me.

I didn't want to come alone. I put my mouth on his nipples and imitated his actions. I took his pulsing cock in my hands and held it firmly as I slid my hand up with the other hand to follow. I stroked him again and again. I was so into his pleasure I forgot about my own.

He suggested to me through labored breaths and his highly aroused state that we should lay down next to the fire. He guided me a few steps and laid me on the rugs and we held each other and kissed. I was ready to love him and so I pushed him to his back and climbed on top of his waiting erection. The pleasure from the pressure of him sliding into me gave me a desire to ride him and make us come. I was on my knees with my hands on his shoulders. I pumped my hips up and down and rocked them back and forth at a frenzied pace. I could feel my orgasm landing in the center of my soul and spreading to every part of me. He started moving his hips in time with mine. His legs tensed and I knew we were both about to explode. We raced to the end and then slowed our pace to slowly enter the realm of good feeling and enjoy each and every second.

I lay on top of him with him still inside of me. We were both out of breath form the ride we took. I looked in his eyes and he into mine. He kissed my lips with two short pecks and then we drifted off to sleep in each other's arms. And to think this all started with a kiss.

WHEN WE GET MARRIED

Anne couldn't believe that the past year culminated in this. She was Mrs. Anne Jordan. She and Joe had a whirlwind courtship. They met, were dating, then engaged and married in one year.

Anne sat on the edge of the bed in their honeymoon suite rubbing her aching feet. She thought they would never leave the reception. One to many well wishers had stepped on her toes. Her face hurt from smiling and her back was tired from standing all day. Joe was in the shower already. She had told him to go first because she couldn't move.

Anne hadn't heard the water stop when she noticed Joe standing in the bathroom doorway in his robe. "Honey, I started your bath. Why don't you let me help you out of your gown and then you can climb into the tub." Anne looked up at the caring man she fell in love with. She thought how loving and attentive he was and loved him even more.

Joe sat behind her on the bed and massaged her neck and shoulders. Anne could feel herself relaxing. Joe started the buttons at her neck and then moved to the zipper. Joe kissed every piece of skin he exposed as he unzipped. Anne could feel the start of butterflies in the pit of her stomach. She let her arms go to her side and the bodice of her gown dropped in the front. Her shoulders and the top of her breasts were exposed. Joe unhooked the connections of her bra and slid his arms around her rib cage from behind to cup her breast.

Anne was so tired that she was torn between her hot bath and making love with her husband. Her 'husband'.

55

She couldn't believe they were married. She also didn't expect to be so tired on her honeymoon. She wanted to start tonight like she planned to participate in the rest of her marriage. She wanted to make love all night long and make tonight memorable.

Anne stopped Joe before things went much further. She said, "Honey, let me take my soak in the tub and then we can pick things up where we left off. I need to unwind a little." Joe helped out of her gown and looked at his beautiful wife. She stood before him in her garter, stockings, and thong panties, looking sexy and sweet. He wanted to hold her in his arms and make her moan. He could feel himself becoming aroused by this thought. Joe said, "The tub should be ready for you by now. Come on and let me wash your back."

Anne rose and walked to the elaborate honeymoon suite bathroom with Joe following behind and watching her ass in her thong. The room was illuminated by candlelight. There were lit candles around the vanity and Jacuzzi/tub for two. Rose petals floated on top of the scented, bubbly water in the tub. A bottle of champagne and two glasses were besides the tub.

Anne looked back at Joe and said, "Honey, you've outdone yourself. When did you have time to get this together?" Joe looked into his wife's dark brown eyes and saw the beginning of tears. As he wiped away a teardrop that rolled down her cheek, he said, "I wasn't really taking a shower. I had the hotel staff bring everything into the bathroom before we got here. I've been in here getting everything ready. Do you like?" Anne looked at Joe and asked, "Do I like?!? I love! I love you and what you've done. You know how much I adore a long soak in the tub. This is a bathaholic's dream come true."

Anne turned to Joe and leaned into him and kissed him. She untied his robe and pressed herself to his bare chest. Her nipples grazed his chest hair. Her nipples hardened and she felt the smoldering desire at her core inflame her whole body. Joe's erection lay between them, pressed into her belly. Joe reached for her garter belt and detached them from her stockings. He found the edge of her thong panties and pulled them down her thighs.

Anne stood before Joe in the steam filled room feeling hot and wanton. She stepped away to remove her remaining clothing. She stepped out of he thong and put a foot on the toilet seat to roll down her stocking. Joe stood there transfixed by her every move. He watched her bend over and her could see her pubic hairs between her thighs. He walked up to her and pressed his desire engorged dick to her ass. She gyrated her hips against him and he groaned from deep in his chest.

Anne stood and turned in his arms and began kissing him. Joe could feel her whimpers cross her lips. He opened his mouth to capture each sound and take it into his being. Anne slid her tongue into his mouth and he sucked it. Their mouths foretold the actions their bodies would later repeat. He held her buttocks in his hands and pressed her to him. His heart pounded in his chest.

Anne pulled away from Joe to slip her hands between them. She slid her hand down his belly to his penis and held it firmly, stroking it up from the base and repeating with the other hand. She reached under his balls to the space before his anus. She rubbed it with her finger. Joe moved in her hands. He took her hands from his erection and told her, "Babe, you're moving ahead of me. Let me help you feel good and we can finish this. Let' climb in the tub and enjoy the bubbles."

Joe held Anne's hand as she stepped into the tub. He stepped in behind her as she stood. Joe sat down and pulled Anne to his lap. Anne snuggled in between his leg facing him. She held his dick in her hands and slid her fingers over it. She enjoyed its softness in the water. Through the soft skin she massaged the firmness. Joe reached forward and squeezed her nipples between his fingertips. Anne dropped her head back and scooted closer to him. Their legs were intertwined and their sexual centers confronting each other.

Joe was ready to enter her then, the urgency out of control inside of him, but he wanted to caress her body more. Anne was also ready, and must have read Joe's mind. She slid as close to him as she could with her legs over his. Joe picked her hips up in his hands and pulled her to him. He felt the head of his penis touch her pubis hairs. He pulled her even closer and entered her waiting sex.

Anne moaned with Joe's entry, and started to rock in his hands. Joe used his hands to increase her rhythm. The water swelled around them, unnoticed by either of them. Anne held onto Joe's shoulders to steady her. She could feel her orgasms coming like an approaching train. "Ooh baby, just a little bit more, please. Just a little bit more", Anne chanted in time to their movements as she rode Joe. As Joe held her hips in his hands, he thrust his groin to meet her. Joe took one of her nipples in his mouth, knowing the added sensation would send her over the edge. Just as he was about to explode himself, he could feel the walls of her vagina constrict on his dick. There were waves of contractions that increased in intensity with each millisecond.

Anne dropped her head forward to Joe's shoulder and moaned from deep in her soul, "Ohhh Joe! I'm coming!!

I'm...I'mm... Coming! as she came. Her leap over the edge hurtled Joe's release to its height. He spasmed in Anne's arms as he came.

They held each other in the aftermath and massaged each other's backs. Joe was the first to speak, "Babe, the waters getting cold. Do you want me to run some hot water?" Anne shook her head no, "I just want to get out and lay in bed next to you. The bath can wait until later."

Anne and Joe got out of the tub and dried off. They stepped over their scattered clothes and climbed into bed, snuggling side by side like spoons in a drawer. Anne said, "And here I was worried about finding enough energy to start things off like I wanted to continue them for the rest of our lives." Joe looked at her and his chest rumbled with laughter as he said, "Well I couldn't tell you were too tired by the way you rode me." "Well you know how to bring out the beast in me." Anne said through a yawn. Joe sat up on one elbow and looked at his bride, "We've got the rest of our lives to find all kinds of ways to bring out the beast and the best in one another. Let's get some sleep Mrs. Jordan." as he leaned forward and kissed her goodnight. Anne said through another yawn, "I love you. Good-night Mr. Jordan."

MULTIPLES

I remember the first time I had a multiple orgasm. It was while my lover performed cunnilingus on me, and it was truly memorable.

I had just showered and I had placed one foot on the side of the tub to smooth lotion down my legs. As I worked the lotion in, I felt a cool draft of air across my naked back as my lover entered the bathroom. He stepped up behind me and wrapped his hands around my waist. He bent over to kiss my shoulders. I could feel his semi-erect, naked dick press into my ass. His kisses worked down my spine as his fingers found my nipples. I moaned his name as he worked my now erect nipples between his fingertips. He squeezed and rolled them as his kisses caressed my neck, shoulders and back.

I could feel the juices collecting between my labia. I was rubbing my ass against his now hard dick. He took one of his hands and started stroking the hair of my cunt. He slid his finger between my wet pussy lips. It felt so good that my muscles clamped down on his finger. He slid his finger in and out. He whispered words of his increasing lust for me in my ear. He told me he wanted to taste me. He wanted to drink my juices and suck me until I came. His words were making me hotter and wetter. I started moving my hips in a thrusting motion so I could fuck his finger. He added another finger for my pleasure. I moaned, "Oh baby! Do me good."

Our pace increased. He was hitting my spot with just his fingers. Just as I was about to come, he stopped. He took his fingers out of my wetness. I turned to look at him and groaned, "No baby. Please don't stop." As I was looking at him, he took his wet fingers and put them into his mouth. He sucked them like a lollipop. He bent over and took my hand. He placed my middle finger with his and slid them into my pulsing pussy. I was so wet; my juices were dripping from my hairs. He guided my finger and we stroked to fervor. I was so horny that I was ready to come with just a few strokes. Just as my muscles started to tense for my release, he stopped again. I was in such a sexual haze that all I could think of was killing him, if he didn't let me come soon. I thought I was about to faint from frustration. He stood me up and turned me to face him. He guided our still wet fingers to his mouth. He sucked them simultaneously and then withdrew his to concentrate on mine.

I felt the pressure of his sucking on my finger. I felt his tongue as it worked around my fingertip. As he looked into my eyes, I felt mesmerized. My stomach dropped as if I were riding a roller coaster. My knees felt weak. I told him, "Baby, I felt light-headed. You made all the blood rush to my cunt." He smiled and led me to the bedroom.

He laid me on the bed on my back. He reached down and rubbed my bush. I spread my legs apart for him to join me. I reached for him and he shook his head no. He said, "I want to taste you come." With that, he put his head between my thighs. As I lost sight of his face, I prayed he would let me come this time.

He started by spreading my labia with his tongue. I felt him lick my clit and a spark of pleasure raced through me. His firm, wet tongue worked around my clit. I thought I would lose consciousness before I came. I could hear the blood roaring in my ears. His tongue dipped into my cunt as I felt myself on the incline of my release. The wetness of his mouth made me hotter. It felt like he was giving my clit a French kiss. As his face pressed closer to me, my hips greeted him thrust for thrust. He alternated his attention between my clit and my vagina. As he worked back and forth, I started coming. My thighs quivered uncontrollably. My hips rocked to their own rhythm. He kept his mouth on me stroking me with his tongue. It was so overpowering that I felt shattered into a million pieces.

Just as I thought I was spent, he started sucking my clit. It was aroused and engorged. He sucked it like I would suck his dick. I felt the spasms of another orgasm starting. I breathlessly moaned, "Baby, oh, baby! What are you doing to me?!?"

I was drained, but I couldn't help myself. I wasn't sure I even wanted to. I was begging him to help me, I asked him to stop and then I begged for more. And just as I thought I couldn't take any more he slid a finger inside of me. He started stroking me and sent my body through another spasm of pleasure.

As he brought his head from between my thighs I could still feel my cunt pulsing. The last thing I remember was him sliding on the bed next to me and kissing me with the taste of my come on his lips.

And then I did something I never do, I fell asleep.

PHONESEX

It was late at night, I was alone and missing my lover. I lay in bed and concentrated my thoughts on him. I was hoping that if I concentrated on him, I could cause him to think about me at the same time I was thinking about him. He had been away for a week, and we hadn't made love since a week before he left on a business trip. I'm always extra horny two weeks after my period. I think it's because my body is releasing an egg and it wants to be paired with a sperm.

I was so horny, that the touch of my gown against my bare breast was arousing me. I had relived some of our most sensuous moments in my dreams at night. I would masturbate every night, but it always felt like something was missing. I could hardly wait until he came home in a few days.

My lover called every night to tell me he loved me and to wish me a good night. It was time for his call and so I knew I must be on his mind. Thoughts of him had started me to feel an ache between my thighs. I slid my finger between the lips of my labia and felt the wetness that is always there when I think of him. My finger began to rub my clitoris in a slow stroke that would bring me a release from this ache. I imagined it was his hand that caressed me. I imagined his tongue licking my erect nipples.

Just as I felt the wetness grow between my thighs, the phone rang. It was him, I just knew it. I answered the phone and was surprised by the breathlessness of my voice as I said hello. I heard him chuckle and he said, "Hello baby. I can tell by your voice that you are thinking of me." He knew that I enjoyed giving myself pleasure. We trusted each other and we were faithful to each other, we also had a very open sexual relationship. We have often played a game where we masturbate in front of each other. Our actions are directed by the instructions of the other. The rule is that there is to be no touching. Whoever made the other touch them in the shortest amount of time won, but then so did the one who got to touch, because we usually made love for hours. So I was not surprised that he knew what I was doing.

I said, "Well, I hope that means you are thinking of me in the same way." I heard him moan a deep, almost growl into the phone. That was my answer; he definitely had me on his mind. I said, "I was just dreaming you were here with me. I could almost feel you sucking my nipples. I could feel the cool air against one nipple as you left it to put your mouth on the other one."

I heard him take in a deep breath. I knew I was getting to him. I told him, "Baby. I am rubbing my finger where you like to put your tongue. You should feel the wetness. I am so wet for you. Only you can do this to me." I heard him moan my name. At that moment I felt a feminine power that was very arousing. I could feel myself getting more turned on as I heard his deep breathing. I didn't know it then, but I was starting something that was going to become a ritual of great pleasure for us.

My own voice was getting deeper and breathless. I think he sensed that I was getting very aroused. I asked him what he wanted to do to me when he came home and we were alone. I wanted him to talk dirty to me on the phone. He said, "Girl, First I'm going to make you naked. I want to see all of you. I am going to give you a breathtaking kiss that will send your senses whirling. I am going to cup your breast. One in each hand. I am going to flick each nipple with my thumbs. My mouth is going to travel down your neck to between your breasts. I want to be surrounded by you. My tongue will travel to your navel. I will dip it in and out of its depth." and he stopped.

I could barely speak. My mind had raced ahead to what would come next, and he stopped. "What next?" I asked. He said, "What do you want to come next?" I said, "What I want is you here with me. But since I'm all alone I guess I'll have to take care of myself." He asked, "What do you have in mind?"

I had gotten so aroused that I knew I was going to have to do something in order to get some sleep. I had started rubbing my clit with a rhythm that was sure to make me come. I reached into my nightstand drawer and pulled out my vibrator. I told him, "I'm going to make my self come while you're on the phone. I've got my vibrator and I'm going to pretend it's you."

He said, "Mmmm Baby. You know I want to be there. Why are you going to tease me like this?" I said, "Because it feel good." And I started my vibrator to humming. I put it to the mouth of the phone. "Do you hear it? Can you imagine it sliding into m juices? Mmmm. You know how I like it nice and slow. I wish you could see me slide it in."

As I was telling him what I was going to do I was actually doing it to myself. I was amazed at how wet I was. I started moaning and I feel could myself about to come. I said, "Baby I think I'm about to come. Oh, I'm going to come." I wanted to make it last. It felt so good. I wanted to make him come with me across the phone lines. I started visualizing what I would do to him if he were here with me.

I heard him moan my name. I asked him, "Are you hard?" He said, "You know you make me hard as a rock. I'm about to explode." I said, "If I was there I would take your head into my mouth. I would swirl my tongue around it and then take you into my mouth. I would caress your balls. I would stroke you up and down with my mouth. I would caress you with my mouth until you were about to come and then I would straddle you. I would ride you until you couldn't control yourself and you explode."

I could hear him breathing heavy. I asked him, "Are you jagging off? Are you going to come? He moaned, "Yeah baby. Just keep talking. Are you playing with that clit?" "Oh yeah. I'm about to come. Please hurry. Oh baby please come with me."

My head was spinning. I was caressing my clit and playing with my nipples. I was about to come. I could hear him moaning. He said, "I'm coming! I'm coming!" Simultaneously I was saying, "Oh, I'm so wet. I'm coming. I can't stop it. Oh...baby...I'm ...coming!"

And then we both came. And all either of us could hear over the phone lines was our heavy breathing and panting.

He said, "Baby? Are you all right? Are you still there?" I said, "Yeah. Are you all right? Was it as good for you as it was for me?" He said, "You know it was, and you know I love you." I said, "I love you too." He said, "Now, you go to sleep and I'll call you tomorrow night." I said," Do you think we can have a repeat performance? If you can handle it." He said, "Yeah. But let's save something for when I get home. Goodnight." "Goodnight." Click.

SOLO

As I lay in bed naked, the morning after we've made love, all I can think about is the next time I can have you between my thighs. I lay there thinking about the ways you make me come. I rub my thumbs across my nipples and they both become hard. As I rub my thumbs back and forth across my nipples, I imagine you sucking them and scraping them with you teeth. I squeeze them between my thumb and index finger sending waves of pleasure to the core of my womanhood. I move the palms of my hands across my nipples in a circular pattern, which adds to my increasing arousal.

My heart rate increases and my breath become shallow. I can smell your cologne in my pillows and on my skin from last night. The smell of our sex still lingers in the air and my head is spinning with images of you ready to fuck me. I moan your name as if you are here with me.

My hands caress down my breast, across my abdomen and stop where my pubic hairs begin. My middle finger slides between the hairy lips that protect my nub of pleasure. My finger slides through remnants of the wetness that you left behind last night and mixes with the juices my efforts today have created. I find my clitoris and rub my finger back and forth across it with smooth, quick movements.

I feel a lightening bolt in the bottom of my stomach. My thighs quiver with pleasure and a desire for a powerful release. I hear myself moaning your name and imagine you are here with me. I move one hand to my breast to fondle my nipples. I squeeze and stroke them alternately.

I dream about giving you pleasure by sucking your dick and caressing your balls. I need you to bury your hardness into my wet pussy. The urgency of my movements increases. My hips rock as if you were here with me. I know that if you were here I would be coming by now. I feel as if something is missing. There is a void in my vagina.

I reach into my nightstand drawer and grab my vibrator. I turn it on. I can feel its vibrations in my hand. I slide its tip against my clit. I rub it back and forth. My body responds to the new pleasures. My temperature is rising. My hips meet the thrusts of the vibrator. I slide it deeper into my waiting cunt, teasing its walls. It feels like a knot is tightening inside of me. One hand moves the vibrator back and forth and the other hand plays with my clit. I wish I could suck my own nipples. I need more. I imagine you setting the pace for our lovemaking. I feel myself holding back so that we can come together.

I feel myself coming. I'm anxious to get there. I dream of feeling your weight on top of me, and you driving your dick into my wetness. I'm almost there. I imagine you sucking my nipples in the shower and you rubbing my body with the loofa sponge. I hear you calling my name as you are coming. I feel like I'm at the top of a roller coaster and I'm about to drop for the ride of my life. My stomach falls as I come. I feel the flood of release, but I still feel unfulfilled. I lay there about to drift off into a light sleep.

The doorbell rings. It's you. I grab a robe and let you in. I know you can smell the essence of sex in the room. I tell you I was just masturbating with thoughts of you. You ask what I was doing. I can see the look in your eyes that tells me you are aroused.

Instead of telling you, I give you your own private showing of how I give myself the pleasure when you're not here. You watch, but before I come again you are nude and making passionate love to me. I find out what was missing all along when we come together. It was you.

Chrystine Dier

<u>STRANGERS</u>

It was Thursday night and had been forever since I had been out. I had a three-day weekend and I wanted to make the most of it. I was suppose to meet Janiece and Claudia at the club, but both of them came up with last minute excuses. I decided to be daring and go alone. My life had been going down a boring, predictable path for the last six months and I was in need of a change.

Janiece, Claudia and I had frequented Charlie's before we got into the hectic lifestyles we were living. It had been longer than I could remember since the last time I had hung out there. It used to be our spot and we went there every Thursday night. We went on Thursdays because of the live jazz band and there wasn't the Friday night crush of those waiting to be chosen and those wanting to choose. It was a comfortable size crowd of people hanging out listening to some live music, engaging in pleasant conversation and dancing to a slow songs without all that jumping up and down and sweating. Well, those days were over because Claudia had gotten married and Janiece was soon to follow since she met Mr. Right. So, I'm off to Charlie's alone.

What to wear? I wanted to feel sexy and so I take a long hot shower and use my favorite cologne at all my pulse points. As I stand in front of my closet I realize that my wardrobe has taken a turn toward the ultraconservative. I find a splash of orange that catches my eye and I pull out a silk wrap around skirt and matching blazer. The skirt is just short enough to show off my legs, and leave room for the imagination. I'm feeling bold and decide to wear the blazer without a blouse. Just the right amount of cleavage is exposed. I put on a garter belt and stockings, and leave

70

the panties behind. I find the matching mules and my outfit is complete.

It's just warm enough not to need a coat. I go to my car feeling like I'm looking my best. The warm night air mixed with my scent heightens my awareness. The excitement of doing something daring is acting as an aphrodisiac. My secret under my skirt is making me feel bold. This started as a night out to change my routine, but who knows what will happen.

I arrive at the club and have the valet park my Acura. I know I'm looking good and the valet couldn't keep his eyes off me. I decided to flash a bit of my thigh as I got out of the car. I walk in the door and pay the cover and see that Danette, a local talent on her way to the top is singing tonight. If nothing else, the music will be great.

As my eyes adjust to the light I see some familiar faces. I see Ron the bartender is still here, as I make my way to the bar. I speak to those familiar faces as I pass. Ron is very charismatic and has a memory that makes everyone feel as if they are his favorite customers. He calls out my name as I approach the bar even though it has been months since he has last seen me. He asks how I am doing and where I have been. I notice that he has already made my rum and coke with a twist of lime as he slides it in front of me. I smile as I thank him for his thoughtfulness. I reach in my purse to pay for my drink and he stops me. He tells me the drink is from an admirer and nods his head toward a gentleman sitting in the corner booth. I turn and smile, raising my glass and mouthing the word thanks.

The gentleman who sent the drink rises and comes over to the bar. As he stands I notice that he must be at least six feet tall. He's that dark chocolate brown that has always turned me on. He has a low haircut, which is more to my taste than these blowouts, a rerun from the seventies that should have stayed there. He has broad shoulders, big muscular arms and large strong looking hands. He has very muscular arms and chest, and a flat stomach that looks as if it has done more than a few sit-ups. He's got an ass to die for that looks great in his pants. His thighs look rock solid. His clothes fit him as if they were custom made.

He walks over to me like a panther on the prowl. I feel as if my assets have just been inventoried. I feel a warmth between my thighs like never before. I'm worried that he is going to ruin the mood by giving a tired pick up line. He asks my name. Now it is my turn to come up with something witty to say. Trying to appear cool and buy some time, I ask him to tell me his name first. He smiles and says his name is Justin. I say "Okay Justin. My name is Chrystine." He asks me to join him at his table. I look around and don't see anyone that I want to sit with and decide this will add to the adventure of the night, and agree to join him. I wink at Ron and join Justin.

Well, so much for appearing cool, as I grin like the Cheshire Cat in Alice In Wonderland. We walk back to his table in the V.I.P. section that gives you a great view of the band, but cloaks you in darkness and provides a bit of privacy in a busy nightclub. The booth could actually accommodate more than the two of us, but his size seems to fill the space. He seats me and then slides in closely beside me. I feel the warmth of his body and smell his cologne and a thrill goes through my body. It takes a great effort to prevent my body from actually trembling.

He whispers in my ear that he saw me as soon as I entered the club and knew that he wanted to be close to me. H e takes my hand in his and I feel my heart skip a beat. His thumb is stroking the back of my hand in a circular pattern that is hypnotizing. Just the feel of his skin against mine makes me want to get closer to him. My breath seems short and my mouth suddenly becomes dry. I take a sip of my drink. As I remove the glass from my lips he takes his finger and touches the wetness on my lips. My tongue darts out to taste his fingertip. He stares into my eyes as if to read my thoughts. I try to determine what I really am thinking, but my head is swimming from the mood of the moment and maybe from my drink.

I sit comfortably cuddled in his arm. He takes his other hand and rubs the silk of my skirt against the nylon of my stockings across my leg. I have always been aroused by touch and enjoy the feeling that the friction is creating. His hand moves under the edge of my wrap around skirt. I feel a wetness growing between my thighs. My heart rate increases with the thought of what he will discover if his hand goes any further. I squirm in my seat to separate my thighs. He takes my movement as an invitation to go further. He looks into my eyes as if to seek my consent. I boldly look him in his eyes as if to say, "Only if you're man enough". He grins and nods his head as if to say "ready or not here we go".

I wait to see the look in his eyes when he realizes that I am not wearing any panties. His hand moves under my skirt and makes contact with the edge of my stocking and the strap of my garter belt. The entire time our eyes are locked together. His hand inches further and comes in contact with my pubic hairs. His hand stops and I watch his eyes. His only facial expression is his left eyebrow raising just a fraction. I'm sitting there trying to appear cool when all I want to do is to open my legs wider and invite him in. He runs his fingers through my hairs and applies the very slightest pressure to my clitoris. I'm trying to keep a normal expression on my face. I start to worry that someone might see what we are doing. The thrill of possibly getting caught adds to the excitement.

My breath seems to be coming in short, shallow puffs. I'm looking at him for some sign of arousal and place my hand in his lap. I am pleased to feel his erection. I am glad to discover that he is not as in control as he would like to appear. As my hand makes contact with his hard penis, he moans from deep in his throat. I feel my nipples harden with the power I realize that I have over him. He looks at my breast just as my nipples are making an impression on my blazer. I look him in his eyes and I slowly run my tongue across my upper lip and then lick my lips as if in slow motion. I caress his erection through the fabric of his pants.

Justin spreads apart my labia to find the core of my pleasure. I feel as if I want to scream. I use my other hand to release his belt and open his zipper. I find to my surprise that he has on silk boxers. I have always loved a man in boxer shorts, and silk must be the most sensual fabric to touch. I hear him take in a breath as I rub the silk of his shorts against his erection. I cannot believe what I am doing in a public place and tell him so. He chuckles and tells me to sit back and enjoy the ride.

I spread my legs even further to give him better access. I use one hand to support myself and the other to continue to give his magnificent erection the attention it deserves. He has a long, thick penis that gives you that full feeling you get as the man enters you. All I can think of is how I am going to get him inside of me. My mouth is watering to taste him but if I were to duck under the table, it might seem obvious. I tell him how much I want to please him. He just says it will come in time.

As we were giving each other our undivided attention our drinks must have gotten low. I reached for my glass to wet my throat and discovered it empty. Almost as if reading my mind Ron approaches our table with drinks. I thank him, but I cannot look him in the eyes. I know that he must have seen what we were doing if he noticed our glasses were empty. Totally embarrassed, I asked Justin if he would like to dance. They are playing a nice slow song. I am hoping we will cool off some. Justin adjusts his pants as I adjust my skirt. He takes my hand and leads me to the dance floor. As we walk to the dance floor I feel like we have everyone's attention. Justin takes me in his arms and pulls me close to him. I feel his erection press against my abdomen. I think that this may not have been such a good idea. He whispers in my ear that he wants to make love to me on the dance floor. I feel a pressure in my vagina and want him to feel the juices he has stirred with his words of lust. We finish the dance and seemed more aroused than before we started.

We head back to our table and he takes a detour. We go down a corridor past the restrooms and through a door. On the other side of the door is an office. Justin takes me in his arms and kisses me passionately. I cannot remember ever having someone kiss me and express so clearly how much he desire me. His lips are full and he seems to rob me of my breath. I breathe in the air he breathes out and feel his power. He opens his mouth and I open mine to taste him. H e holds my breast in his hands and rubs his thumbs across my hard nipples. He presses his pelvis into mine and lets me know how much he wants me. I feel more excited than I have ever felt in my life. I pull my lips from his and ask him "Who's office is this? What if we get caught?" He tells me not to worry and kisses me to mindless oblivion. His hands run up my thighs under my skirt. He slips his finger between my wet lips and caresses my clitoris. I moan my pleasure. I begin to unfasten his pants to have direct contact with his skin. His penis jumps out of his pants at me. I hold it between my hands and can almost feel it pulsing. He moans "Oh Chrystine. That feels so good baby. I knew when I saw you that you would be magic."

He takes my hand and leads me to the desk across the room. This is the first time that I notice there is a desk in the center of the room with an armed leather chair. He lowers his pants and sits in the chair. He tells me to straddle him. I am on my knees above his waiting cock. I am so wet that as I slide down on him, we fit like in a glove. I settle on his erection and just enjoy the feeling of fullness. The feeling gets so good that I cannot wait and begin to move up and down, stroking him with the walls of my vagina. I let my thighs control the rhythm. He matches me stroke for stroke. The intensity and pace increase. I am breathing heavy and I feel a tightening in my cunt. It feels like the assent on the highest peak of a roller coaster. We continue to climb. He opens the front of my blazer and unfastens the front closure of my bra. My breast spill out and he takes a nipple in his mouth. I can feel him suck and nibble at my nipple. He grabs my ass to help direct the rhythm as I hold the back of the chair.

We rock the chair and I am sure it is going to topple over just as I reach the edge of my release. We increase the pace even more. I tell him I am about to come, but I want to wait for him. He tells me, "Baby, I'm almost there. Wait for me." Just when I don't think I can wait I feel his penis pulse and feel his juices shoot inside of me. The force of his come pushes me over the edge and I come. I collapse on top of him. I almost feel embarrassed, but the after glow of great sex tells me it was well worth it.

I rise off his cock and settle my feet on the floor as I adjust my skirt. He stands and zips his pants. I tell him that I am going to the restroom to freshen up, and I will meet him at the table. I look out of the office door before slipping out. As I leave I blow Justin a kiss. I decide to go home and make a pleasant close to a passionate evening, so I pass the restroom as I head toward the door. I wave to Ron as I weave my way through the crowd. As I wait outside for the valet to bring my car I look back and see Justin move toward the table. As he sits down and looks around the room we make eye contact just as my car arrives. I hesitate, but get in my car and drive home.

I feel the cool night air against my skin as I replay the night's events in my mind. I decide to take the scenic route home. I can smell his cologne on my skin and I feel myself getting aroused with the thoughts of his touch. I pull up in front of my house and park my car. When I enter my apartment I hear sounds of Will Downing playing. I kick off my shoes and walk to the bathroom. I walk in to find the tub filled with my favorite bubble bath. There are candles lit around the room. I turn around to smile at my lover who made it home before me. Justin is standing in the doorway with a towel around his hips. In each hand he holds a glass of sparkling wine. He smiles at me and says, "That was pretty tricky of you to leave without saying good-bye. I had more surprises up my sleeve to share with you." I said to him, "That just gives us something to try next time we meet and pretend not to know each other." As I start taking off my clothes I ask, "How did you get Ron to play along with our secret rendezvous?" He said, "I told him there would be a bonus in his check if he kept everyone away from my office."

As I slide into the tub with a sigh he hands both glasses to me. He slides in behind me and wraps his big strong arms around me. I lay my head back on his chest and sip from my glass. I say, "I thought we were going to use different names. When I asked you your name, you were suppose to say 'Jordan, just like Michael.'" He Says, "I know, but when I saw how sexy you looked I could barely remember my own name, let alone some make believe name." He asks, "I thought you were going to have Claudia and Janiece with you?" I say, "They both had other plans, but you know they would not have stood for playing along with another one of our love games."

I snuggle back against his hips and feel his satin soft, wet, erect penis against my back. I ask, "Do you have some thing for me?" He chuckles and says, "Yes, just a continuation of where we left off when you slipped out the door on me." I sit the glasses on the floor and turn to face him as I splash water everywhere. He looks me in the eyes and says, "Chrystine, you are the sexiest woman I have ever known and I love you. You bring all the excitement to a romance that any man could ever ask for. I want to make love to you, and with you until my dying days." With tears in my eyes I tell him, "Justin, I will always love you and because I do, my mind is filled with thoughts and ideas to keep our days together exciting. You turn me on when you look at me and just touch me.

I love you so much that it makes me happy to keep you happy." I stand and grab a towel from the heated towel rack. Justin stands in front of me and steps out of the tub. He wraps me in the towel and carries me to our bedroom. Our bedroom is lit with candlelight and our bed is covered with rose petals. He whispers in my ear as he lies down, "Life with you has been a bed of roses." He kisses my lips and lies on top of me. His erection presses between my thighs. I feel my internal warmth rise as he nibbles at my neck. I open my legs to grant him access to the wonders of my world. As he slides into me he moans my name. I start the rhythm that has guided our passion. I am so ready for him and him for me that there are no word spoken, just the conversation between our bodies. As I feel myself coming, I feel him increase the pace. He knows my body so well. I hold back waiting for him to join me at the edge. I see the sweat on his brow and know that we will both take the plunge over the edge very soon. Just as I feel myself come, I feel him come inside of me. Between breaths he says, "Chrystine...I...Love...You..."

At that moment all is right in the world. He rolls away and covers us up. He holds me in his arms and we fall asleep.

TASTE

It was a cold winter evening, and Julia lay in the tub wishing Carl would get home. It was her routine to have a long soak in the tub on Sunday evening to get ready for the workweek grind. I was her time to pamper herself. She had the lights down low and was listening to Michael Franks on the CD player. She was up to her neck in bubbles with her inflated bath pillow behind her head.

As she lay there enjoying the warm water caressing her body, she was fantasizing about Carl being in the tub behind her and caressing her breast. Julia could feel her nipples tighten as she visualized his fingers on her skin. She could feel stirrings of desire between her thighs. Julia twirled her fingers around each nipple, increasing her arousal. She reached one hand under the water to slip her finger over her clit. She moved her finger back and forth over its' nub. "Mmmm that feels good" crystal thought as she felt the warm waters moving across her labia.

Julia was enjoying the pleasure she was giving herself. She was remembering the night before when she and Carl made love. She imagined his mouth sucking her nipples and making them wet. She could feel a tightening in her belly. She felt the beginnings of an orgasm. She had to stop herself because she wanted to save it for Carl. She ached between her thighs.

Julia got out of the tub and toweled off. The terry cloth across her nipples tightened the ache. As she dried off she slipped her finger inside her labia and felt how wet and reedy she was for Carl. She hoped he came home soon.

Julia went into the bedroom. She wanted put on some lotion and to find something sexy to wear. As she sat on the edge of the bed applying the lotion she heard Carl come into the apartment. He walked into the bedroom to see Julia sitting naked on the bed applying lotion to her arms and breast. "Mmmm baby. You smell good and look good enough to eat", he said as he leaned in for a kiss.

Julia looked up at Carl with desire in her eyes. She was already wet and aching for him. He told her, "Move back in bed and let me rub your body down with that lotion." Julia sat back into the center of their king size bed. Carl took the lotion from her and poured it into his hand. He reached for her right foot and smoothed it up the front of her calf and down the back of it. He lifted her foot up higher and Julia tumbled onto her back. Carl leaned forward and kissed her toes. Julia moaned. Carl looked at her and said, "I like the red polish on your toes. Did you do that just for me?" Julia gave a husky "*yes*".

Carl kissed her inner calf and stopped at the knee. He placed her right leg down and picked up her left foot. He rubbed the lotion on her left calf and then kissed his way from her toes to her knees. Julia was so ready for him she thought she was going to come from just his kisses. Carl kneeled forward onto the bed and spread apart Julia's knees. He could see how wet and ready she was for him. He couldn't wait to use his tongue to separate her hairs covering her essence of womaness. He wanted to slip his tongue over and around her clit.

Julia remained on her back. She had a handful of the sheets in each hand. She was spinning out of control with desire and needed to hold on. Carl leaned between her knees and kissed her inner thighs. One kiss at a time, he moved from thigh to thigh and moved forward. He stopped at her tattoo of a heart with his name in it. It was one kiss away from his destination. He licked it and then kissed his way around the heart. Julia was moving her hips, trying to get closer to his mouth. Carl was not going to move ahead any sooner than he wanted. He was in control. He moved just a little bit more to claim his prize. Julia was calling his name, "Carl. Oh Baby. Carl I need you. Help me." Julia was so ready from him she thought she was going to come from his breath moving her hairs.

Carl reached the hood of her clit by separating her pubic hairs with his tongue. His hot breath was coming faster. Julia could feel it on her skin. Her nipples were hard and she reached to stroke them. Carl stroked her clit with his tongue. He would make his tongue hard and act as if her were dueling with her clit. Then he would make it soft and flutter his tongue across it. Julia's hips were moving with his tongue. She wanted to press her cunt closer to his mouth, but wanted to make this last longer.

Carl dipped his tongue into her pussy and Julia felt a jolt that went from her pussy in two directions. It went to her head and her toes. Julia moaned, "Oh baby. Do it to me. You feel so good." Carl gave her cunt a kiss and started tonguing it. Julia was out of her mind. She could feel the beginnings of an orgasm. She was moving her hips with every stroke of his tongue.

Carl dick was hard and wanted out of his clothes. Carl continued to move his tongue from Julia's clit to the opening of her vagina. He started to remove his pants. He thought is strange, but he was jealous of his own tongue. He wanted to sink his dick into Julial's wetness. Just as he had his pants unfastened and down his thighs he could hear Julia saying she was coming. "Baby...Carl...Ohhh...Baby...Mmm...I'm...Commming" as her thighs began to quiver. Carl focused his attention on her clit as Julia came. Hearing her moaning as she came was making him harder. Carl wanted to be inside of her.

Julia was short of breath as Carl lay on top of her. "Baby that felt so good" Julia said as she kissed his lips. She could taste herself on his lips. She could feel his hard dick between her thighs. Just knowing he was hard was making her ready for him. "Baby. I want to be inside of you." Carl said as he kissed her nipple. Julia loved him to suck her nipples. He knew it and it was making he hot. Julia opened her thighs to welcome him. Carl's dick dropped between her thighs and was nestled against her wet pubic hairs. Carl rose up on his hands and Julia took his hard dick and guided it into her. She was so wet, but Carl was so hard. He slid into her and felt his gut tightening. He slid in and out for a few strokes. He moaned her name, "Mmm Julia. Baby you always feel so good to me." His pace quickened and Julia felt herself about to come again. She wanted to wait for him. Carl started moving quicker with shorted thrusts and Julia knew he was almost there. She took her own nipple in her mouth for him to see. Carl looked at her sucking her own nipple and started to feel himself coming. "Ohh girl. Ohh baby. Mmm. I'm...coming." Julia let herself go and they came together.

Carl lay on top of Julia and kissed her lips. As he lay there he realized he loved every taste of her. From her head to her toes, and anywhere he stopped along the way. Carl got undressed. They lay in bed together tasting each other and Julia said, "Okay, now it's my turn to taste you." Carl smiled and they started all over again.

YOHIMBE

Melissa was so angry, frustrated and horny that she thought she would explode. She couldn't understand why she had a man, was in a committed relationship, but was always wantin' some dick. It wasn't like she had an unusually high sex drive. She considered herself to be normal, just like her friends. They were all thirty something women with stress filled lives, who wanted some good lovin', a big firm dick between their thighs on a regular basis, a little TLC from that someone special, and someone you can love who loves you.

She and some of her girlfriends had gotten together for drinks after work today. The conversation leant its self towards more talk about men and sex. The main subject was about an aphrodisiac for men that one of the girls had tried on her man and met with much success. It was called yohimbe and was the rage in the health food industry. It was an herb made from a tree bark found in West Africa. It was suppose to be able to give your man energy and make him keep it up all night long.

Melissa was truly horny and hadn't been able to keep Mike awake long enough to help him get it up. He was a good man who worked really hard, and they had a good relationship. They shared many common interests and enjoyed each other's company. She couldn't complain that he never gave her enough attention, but he was always tired. She could trust him with her heart and soul; just not count on him for a regular orgasm. It was good when he gave it, as a matter of fact it was great, but with the hours he put in at work he never seemed to have enough time or energy.

Melissa had tried enticing him with sexy lingerie and erotic stories by this new author that was known for her steamy couple oriented erotica named Chrystine Dier. She had tried seducing him by arriving at his office nude under her fur coat, and by putting nude pictures of herself in his briefcase. She even tried making their own pornographic video of the two of them while making love to replay and let him see how good they were together. Each of her attempts worked for the moment, but nothing had worked long term.

Melissa was ready for some hot, bed board bangin' against the wall, all night long, sweatin' your hair out and slidin' up and down each other sex. She was ready for whatever this yohimbe promised to do. She stopped at a health food store her girlfriend recommended called HY-TEK Nutrition. She wasn't quite sure what she was looking for and was too embarrassed to ask. After roaming around the store for a while and ordering a fresh vegetable juice drink from the juice bar, she found the male virility and energy section. Melissa was looking through the section when she found it, YOHIMBE. It was clearly marked on several bottles of different brands.

After making her choice she paid for her items and left the store with a skip in her step. The next thing was to get Mike to take it. Melissa chose the liquid because she thought it would be easier to give to Mike unnoticed. You were supposed to take two droppers full in a drink. Mike always had to have his morning juice, so it should be no problem to put it in there.

The next morning Melissa put Mike's breakfast on the table with his juice besides his plate. Mike didn't even seem to notice anything different as he drank his juice. Mike grabbed his briefcase and prepared to leave for work.

Mike looked at Melissa and said, "Baby, I'll be home a little late from work so you don't have to wait up for me tonight." Melissa smiled and said, "I'll be waiting. You know I can't sleep unless I know you are home safely." Beside Melissa hoped the yohimbe would have some effect by then.

Melissa came home from work tired. She decided to take a long soak in the tub and be ready for Mike when he came home. She checked the answering machine and found a message from Mike. He said that he finished up sooner that he thought and would be home on time. He sounded more energetic than usual and very up beat. Maybe he just had a good day or the yohimbe was working.

Melissa lounged in the tub and took extra care in getting ready. She had a bottle of sparkling grape juice chilling in the frig and had changed the bed linen to their satin sheets. She pulled out one of Mike's favorite pieces of lingerie. It was the one with no crotch and the push up bra. Even if it was a little uncomfortable, Melissa knew she shouldn't be in it for long.

Just as she was lighting the last candle in the bedroom she heard Mike's key in the door. She could feel her blood rush to her cunt in anticipation of what may come, and hopefully who would come. She was already wet and ready for him to slide into her. She looked forward to the thought of foreplay, but not too much, she was ready to get down to business. Mike called out her name and she told him she was in the bedroom. When he walked in and saw her in his favorite lingerie he smiled and said, "You must be a mind reader. I couldn't get the sight of you in that out of my mind all day. And I come home to find you in it. "Melissa just smiled. She couldn't believe she was getting these kinds of results already.

Mike walked to her and kissed her lips and slid his lips down the side of her throat. Melissa could feel her nipples tighten. She reached forward and felt his erection through his pants. Mike started to shrug his shoulders out of his jacket and let it drop to the floor. He reached for Melissa's waist and pulled her to him and pressed his hips into her. It reminded her of when they used to grind while slow dancing. Mike remembered too, and felt how good she felt in his arms. He couldn't let the job get so much of his time that he forgot what was important and what felt good.

Mike slid his hands up her sides to her belly and then to her breast. He felt her erect nipples under his fingertips. He could feel his heart pounding in his chest and his blood roaring in his ears. He felt hotter than he could ever remember. He wanted to just throw Melissa on the bed and take her. His mind was spinning with thoughts of being on top of her, inside of her. Stroking in and out of her wetness. He heard Melissa moan as he was rolling her nipples between his fingertips.

Melissa started to unbutton the front of his shirt. She wanted to feel his skin close to hers. Melissa felt air on her breast. Mike had released them from their push up confinement. He bent forward to suckle her nipples as she pulled his shirt from his arms. Melissa arched her breast toward his lips. Mike moaned as he sensed her urgency.

Mike stepped back, guiding her body with his hands, to the edge of the bed. He sat down with Melissa standing in front of him. Her navel was in front of him and he had the urge to dip his tongue inside and take a taste. He pulled her straps off her shoulders and moved her teddy to her waist. He reached between he thighs and felt her pubic hairs. That's why he loved her crotchless panties, easy access. He slid his finger between her slit and felt her wetness. He could smell her sex and arousal. He was intoxicated by her scent and aroused to a burning point.

Melissa rocked her pelvis to encourage his fingers sliding in further. Mike wanted out of his pants. He needed to be inside of her to give her what she craved, what he needed. He stood and removed his pants. His erection was pressed against his belly. Melissa took his briefs off and he stepped out of them.

Melissa knelt at his feet to take his brick hard dick into her mouth. She cradled his balls in her hand and used the other hand to stroke his length. She wrapped her lips around his stiff rod and licked as if there was melting ice-cream dripping down the sides.

Mike couldn't take anymore. If he didn't enter her wet pussy soon he was going to come in her face. He couldn't seem to control himself. He hadn't felt like this since he was a teenager. Mike reached down and pulled Melissa to her feet. She slid up against the length of him. Mike turned her to the bed and laid her down. She lay before him with her legs spread apart. Mike could see the wetness dripping from her hairy lips. He couldn't decide to lick her or sink into her. Mike knew he couldn't wait any longer and Melissa didn't look as if she could either.

Melissa lay on the bed reaching her arms out for him. She squirmed on the bed and moaned to him to come to her because she needed him. Mike kneeled on the bed and positioned himself between her thighs. As he slid into her, he felt the room spin and all the blood leave his brain. He was going on autopilot. His stoke went back and forth while he rubbed her clit. Melissa matched him stroke for stroke. Melissa was so excited she thought she would lose control. Mike felt like a teenage boy getting his first piece.

He was about to come and couldn't control himself enough to ensure that Melissa was satisfied.

Mike knew he about to hit the point of no return and then he heard Melissa say, "Oh baby! Oh baby! I'm...about...to...commme. I can't wait! Give it to me deep!" That's all Mike needed to hear. He gave it to her deep and long, just enough to send him over the edge. Mike groaned as he shot his load into Melissa. He felt Melissa's velvet walls clamp down on his pulsing cock. He couldn't believe how invigorated he felt.

Melissa lay there feeling like a rag doll. She moved up to the top of the bed and Mike followed and lay beside her. He looked at her and smiled, "Girl, that was awesome. Let's get started again." Melissa said, "Whoa, champ. I need a moment to regroup." Mike said, "Not you who has been begging for it every night. I can't believe I'm ready before you." Melissa looked at him shyly and said, "There's a reason for that. I gave you some yohimbe in your juice this morning. It's supposed to act as an aphrodisiac and give you energy. I found out about it from some of the girls at work."

Mike looked at her in shock, "You gave me some yo-what?! Are you trying to poison me? That's the thanks I get for working hard?" "Calm down sweetheart, it is yohimbe, a natural herb from a tree in West Africa. It can't hurt you. And it surely helped. Don't you feel energized, even after great sex?" Mike had to think, he agreed even if he wasn't ready to admit it. "Well you give that stuff to me and I'll take it when *we* agree that it's needed. Besides from the looks of you laying there so worn out, it looks like you could use some cause I'm ready for some more of that good stuff you've got between your thighs." Melissa smiled and rolled over on top of Mike and said, "I said I

Chrystine Dier

just needed to regroup, not take a nap. I'm ready whenever you are." Melissa straddled Mike's hard dick and they rocked the night away.

The bottle of yohimbe sat in the bedroom and was pulled out whenever one felt the other wasn't keeping up, and they both made use of its potency.

ABOUT THE AUTHOR

Chrystine Dier resides in Chicago, Illinois. She is the mother of one son. She has always had a love of reading. She enjoys romances, mysteries and African-American authors. She has often dreamed of putting her own words on paper and this is her first attempt to become published. She is intrigued by romantic erotica, and decided to try her hand at her own version. When she is not writing she is a registered nurse and nurse practitioner specializing in women's health.